I Solemnly Swear

A Government Frozen by Broken Promises

Dr. Cristina Guarneri

When you are in any contest,
you should work as if there were -
to the very last minute - a chance to lose it.
This is battle, this is politics. This is anything.

— Dwight D. Eisenhower

Author's Note ~

After twenty-two years of campaign experience and research, I have found that up until 2005, there were very few political leaders who could make a positive and lasting impression— not only on policy but on the communities they represented. As an author, it's never a right, but a privilege to write about life. I often need to keep in mind that it's also a sensitive journey for me.

The focus of this book, I Solemnly Swear, shows a new way of reforming leadership in politics and keeping with the solemn vow taken on oath when entering public office. The need for political reform is a necessary first step to maintaining democracy in our government system.

With a new way of thinking and doing business, reform politicians can become leaders that wouldn't compromise their ethics, not even under the prestige of power and politics. Instead, achievement can come out through hard work, commitment, and perseverance as an emerging theme for the United States. Developing reform politicians may seem like unlikely candidates, but sometimes even the most unlikely become some of our greatest leaders. Many reform politicians have lost and have won some important campaigns over the years, but those losses have shaped them into becoming politicians that have been leading the people toward positive change and success while steering away from the political machines of the past that have haunted much of American politics and its history.

I've learned that reform politicians do not just come to learn of their journey overnight. It is instead, a step-by-step process that would bring such leaders to realize their full potential while understanding how time would become a virtue for them to solemnly swear to uphold an oath in public office and to keep it. Being a reformer isn't an easy sell for many who hold government positions. Yet for many people, we seek to find such political leadership. We seek to find those that will make a difference in our lives and fulfill our hopes for a better life— not only for today but for the countless tomorrows that are ahead.

TABLE OF CONTENTS

Author's Note

PART I

PART II

PART III

About the Author

Part I

Chapter One: I Solemnly Swear

Without ethics, man has no future. This is to say, mankind without them cannot be itself. Ethics determine choices and actions and suggest difficult priorities.

—John Berger

I, do solemnly swear that I will uphold the Constitution of the United States and the Constitution of the State of New Jersey and that I will bear true faith and allegiance to the same and the Governments established in the United States and in this State, under the authority of the people and that I will faithfully, impartially and justly perform all of the duties of the office according to the best of my ability. So help me God.

These are the words often heard when taking oath in public office, but they aren't just words, they are the promise that many people believe will be kept. For many who make this solemn vow, the promise to serve others is there. However, the longer that an elected official stays in office, the oath looks more a formality, but not all public servants will view their oath in such a way. Instead, some still hold themselves to a high standard and keep themselves accountable to the words, I solemnly swear.

From his time serving as a U.S. Marine to leading Jersey City as Mayor, Steven Fulop had made it part of his career to always be guided by a strong desire to take on difficult challenges and find solutions that help improve people's lives.

As the son of Jewish immigrants and the grandson of Holocaust survivors, I know how important it is to stand up against hatred, bigotry, and antisemitism in all its forms. That personal family history has always guided my values and my public service, and as Governor to work towards a more just society that treats people of every background with fairness and respect.

According to his 2019 mayoral profile, all four of Steven's grandparents were Holocaust survivors, including a grandmother who was sent to Auschwitz. All four of his grandparents were born in Transylvania, the heavily wooded, mountainous, lushly beautiful region that has changed hands between Hungary and Romania. As this story begins, it still was part of Hungary. World War II came late there; his mother's parents, the Kohns, were taken from the ghetto toward its end. His grandfather, Alexander, went to a transit camp, and his grandmother,

Rosa, was on one of the last transports to Auschwitz in April 1944. A painful story that would be told by family members for decades.

As there were two lines at Auschwitz, one was for the very young and the very old; the other was for people who could work. In between them, making selections, and decreeing death, was Josef Mengele who radiated evil. Mrs. Kohn clutched her 20-month-old baby, Eva, who was about to be sent to the other line. She asked "What would happen to them?" before pointing up to the black smoke fouling the sky. The guard answered, "They are turned into that." She screamed and tried to run, and a guard hit her on the head with a rifle, knocking her out. She survived, and so did her husband. However, the rest of the family, including Eva, did not; Rosa Kohn went on to give birth to Steven's mother, Carmen Kohn Fulop, who was born in Romania in 1954.

The family had been comfortable in Transylvania, but under Nicolae CeauÈ™ Romania went Communist, and the family lost what it had been able to reclaim, what was believed, but untrue, that Steven's grandfather would be badly beaten as goons searched for gold coins they believed him to have hidden. In 1967, the family managed to flee

Romania for Brooklyn, where Steven's grandparents left everything they knew to better their children.

Steven's father, Arthur Fulop, and his family lived in Tg-Mures, a small town about 120 miles from his future wife's home, in a place so remote that war never fully touched it. He was born in 1947, right after its end.

In 1964, the Fulops, who had applied for a passport, were given one – and told that it would be operational for just one week. They left immediately, with almost nothing. After a stop in a transit camp in Rome, they decided to go to Israel. Even though Steven's father had family in the United States, he declined so to go to his country, so they all headed east to Israel. Although, the family's time in Israel was not a success. The nation was in a tough economic bind, and it was not particularly welcoming to newcomers – the chadashim, whom the old-timers, the vatikim, thought of as competition. Steven's grandfather, Bentsi, bought a truck, but the loads that he hoped to haul rarely materialized. After three years, he, his wife, Elizabeth, and their younger son gave up and moved to the United States, where their lives finally grew roots. Steven's father was 18 at the time and had been drafted into the Israel Defense Forces like everyone else his age. Toward the end of his service, the Six-Day War broke out; he was a sniper in the elite Golani Brigade. It was a very hard time for Steven's father, as he saw things that he wished he had not seen. It left him with the strong feeling that war comes from demonizing your opponents rather than allowing yourself to see them as human, and that very little is worth the devastation that such hatred causes.

By the time he was 36 years old, Steven Fulop had one of those jaw-dropping resumes specially reserved for rising politicians. Oxford. NYU Stern. Columbia. Goldman Sachs. The United States Marine Corps. Iraq. Jersey City's youngest-ever city councilman. As the Observer wrote: Steven's biography reads likes Horatio Alger: he grew up in middle-class Edison, N.J., the second of three sons of Israeli and Hungarian immigrants. His parents owned a deli in Newark, where Steve worked as a teenager. His grandparents were Holocaust survivors who the Fulop family says came to America penniless.

In May 2013, Steven was elected mayor of Jersey City. It was a bizarre, special election in which Steven defeated the incumbent, Jerramiah Healy, who had been convicted of obstruction of justice earlier in his mayoral term and refused to resign. Despite this, Steven remained something of an outsider in the race and won without the backing of the political establishment. His critics charge that he's too friendly with Wall Street while his admirers see a striking resemblance between Steven and former Newark mayor and newly minted New Jersey Senator Cory Booker, who is also young, cozy with the finance service industry, and very active on social media.

When his family came to the United States, they brought up their three sons, Daniel, Steven, and Richard in Edison, New Jersey. They thought it was important that Steven have a Jewish education. This led to his attending an Orthodox day school up until the 8th grade. Steven had confessed in an interview with Jersey Journal that it had been kind of a strange experience because his family wasn't religious. He remembered kids would come over to his house and play and he would always have to pretend or hide the Oreo cookies.

Steven's father owned a deli in Newark, down the street from the courthouse. They bought it in 1968, right after the riots when real estate there had become affordable. His mom ran a service bureau for immigrants next door. Both of Steven's parents worked hard. They held dearly to the values of the United States where they could live free and prosperous lives, and are deeply connected to their Jewish roots. They passed on these beliefs to their sons.

Steven, like his brothers, went to the Rabbi Pesach Raymon Yeshiva in Edison, and then to the Solomon Schechter School of Union and Essex, as today's Golda Och Academy in West Orange then was named. He left it in 11th grade for public school, where he could play soccer more seriously. The family belonged to the local Conservative shul, Neve Shalom, and the boys went to Jewish summer camps and USY.

After high school, Steven went to Binghamton University, part of New York State's public college network. He spent his junior year abroad at Oxford University, studying finance at New College. When he got back, he took a job at Goldman Sachs in Chicago, where his older brother already worked. He was hired into asset management with mutual funds, then moved into equity trading.

Goldman moved him back to the New York office in 2000, and Steven bought a condo in Jersey City. Although he was not politically active and not even at that time registered to vote, Jersey City was perfect for him. It was back in New Jersey, close to his parents, right across the river from his job, and booming, so any real estate deal there was likely to be advantageous. Life was good for Steven.

Each day, Steven was at work at 1 New York Plaza in lower Manhattan on September 11, 2001. He felt the building shake when the planes hit. It shook something inside him too. Not long after, he started talking to recruiters meaning armed forces recruiters. Steven didn't know anything when he started. He tried to do the research, to understand the different branches. He asked himself questions: "Do I have to shave my head? Can we figure out some other way so that I don't have to do it? When I asked the recruiters, they said no, it doesn't work that way." Steven went in on the enlisted side. He didn't have to, he could have been an officer in the reserves, but Steven didn't want to commit to what might become four years of active duty, and he was willing to serve right away.

After considering his options, Steven enlisted in the Marines, and soon he found himself in South Carolina, in boot camp on Parris Island. He was 25 years old. He always thought that military service was important, but in the 1990s, it didn't seem relevant. Steven would say to himself that if it ever were necessary for him to do it, he would do it. Then 9/11 happened, and he thought okay. Here we are. It's the crossroads. He was still young enough. He didn't have kids and he was in good shape, so he enlisted.

Only a few months into his first term as mayor, he tackled education reform, and turned Jersey City, the State of New Jersey's second-biggest city, into a medium-sized city whose vigor has been restored by the arrival of young professionals and artists. Jersey City has a lot going for it. It boasts cheap real estate and an unacknowledged proximity to Manhattan. As Tablet contributor Nona Willis Aronowitz wrote:

> It has the dual upsides of being smaller (its population is right around 250,000), cheaper, and more community-oriented than its gargantuan neighbor—yet closer to the tip of Manhattan than some places in Brooklyn and the upper Island. Real estate prices in downtown Jersey City, which has experienced rapid development over the past few years, can rival yuppie Brooklyn's, but residential neighborhoods like Jersey City Heights are starting to entice young people with actual cheap rent, laid-back bars, and a cornucopia of inexpensive ethnic restaurants.

Steven is both as deeply American and as fully Jewish as one person's story could be – it is our 21st-century version of the great American dream.

Steven described in an interview that his parents were distraught when he told them of his entering the military. He was making good money, had a good life, and they were scared for their son.

However, it was their values that attracted Steven to service. Having a lot of appreciation for the United States, he once said that it was his family's sweat equity, and so he viewed his service as a minor down payment on that appreciation. Although it was very complicated and emotional, his parents agreed that Steven follow his heart. His Jewishness accompanied Steven to boot camp. Parris Island, which is notorious for its toughness, and the toughness of the Marines it turns out is very structured.

With every second of every minute of every day being scheduled, the only respite from that is religion, and the Marine Corps honors other religions beyond the basic Christian denominations. Meaning the Marine Corps goes above and beyond to make sure that every person can practice, with the only time that isn't structured being on Sundays when you have religious services. Since there is no Jewish presence on Parris Island, they would bring in a rabbi from Buford, South Carolina. At that time, Steven was the only one there. It was the only time the drill instructors would leave cadets alone. During service time, the rabbi would ask how Steven was doing. He responded by saying that he was starving. The rabbi would ask what it was that Steven wanted, and he replied dessert. So he brought in dessert every week.

With boot camp lasting 13 weeks, Steven's parents attended his graduation. It was the first time they got to see the military culture. After Parris Island, he experienced a culture shock, as he reentered Goldman Sachs. After putting Steven on their homepage, since he presented them with a public relations bonanza, given that the company had just suffered through the terrors of 9/11, Steven was also given real emotional support there. Later, other employees enlisted or joined the reserves, but Steven was the first. There was no model yet for how to handle the situation.

Three months later, in January 2003, he went to Quantico, Virginia, for reserve duty, that's when his commanding officers were going around, asking for all sorts of personal information. Steven recounted their first hearing of his deployment:

After hearing of his dismissal for the weekend, Steven and the others were asked to come back on Tuesday with their powers of attorney and their wills. 'You are being deployed.' At first, Steven was in shock, but at the same time, the inevitable may happen. That was when he went to see his parents at their home in the Poconos. Steven made the decision to drive there on his way home from Quantico. As soon as his mom saw him, she began to cry, she knew what was happening.

Steven's mom said to him to remember that the reason for the American invasion of Iraq was Saddam Hussein's arsenal of weapons of mass destruction. We know now that the arsenal was a figment of overheated imagination, but then we did not. As far as she knew, she was saying goodbye to a son who might be gassed just as surely as the baby sister she never had the chance to meet had been.

Early that Monday morning, Steven went to his office. He went to his desk and wrote an email to everyone he had ever met in his life. In his email, he said, "Friends, family, co-workers, everyone. I say that I am leaving on Tuesday, being deployed, and I want to thank people for being part of my life. "He put on his jacket and even before he had hit 'send' and started to walk out, people began to clap for him and began to cry, and they began to cry too.

It had to be difficult to have a power of attorney and a will, but this is what Steven had with him. That next Tuesday, he flew from Delaware to Camp Pendleton in

California. They put on their gas masks there and waited for three weeks for their equipment. It was from there, that he was flown to Kuwait. President George W. Bush declared his "Shock and Awe" campaign on March 17, and on March 18 Steven and his troop crossed into Iraq. He was in the 6th Engineer Support Battalion, attached to the 1st Marine Division; the battalion's responsibility was building bridges, purifying water, and generally working on infrastructure.

Over Passover, Steven was in Iraq. The rabbi had on a camouflage tallis. He told a story that he said demonstrates the lengths to which the U.S. military will go to respect religion. Steven and the others were living in tents. They hadn't showered for months and there was no internet, no phones, not much of anything. That's when Steven saw a note in his chow hall that there was a religious service on an Army base. Steven asked to go, and they let him. With an escort and security, Steven stated that no other country would go to those lengths to make sure that someone could get to a Seder. Although Steven's time on active duty was short, it was still intense.

Traveling up to Baghdad, he and the others were deployed for six or seven months, then went back to Kuwait, back to Pendleton, and then back home. Within a year, Steven was back at Goldman Sachs. He looked back at his time and felt that he got more out of the Marine Corps as a person and as a human being than it got from him.

Steven stayed at Goldman for a few years and then moved on, pursuing what would have looked like a normal upward career path, the journey someone clearly smart and ambitious would be expected to take. He continued to live in Jersey City, active in his condo association but not involved in politics, but soon he would re-examine the landscape of the City.

When Steven came back to Jersey City, Robert Menendez, the Democrat who is now the state's senior U.S. senator, was his congressman. He also was chair of the House Democratic caucus, the most senior Hispanic federal legislator in the country, and the state's most senior House member. New Jersey's Frank Lautenberg, then a U.S. senator, resigned in 2001 – he ran again and took the state's other seat in 2003 – and everyone assumed that Mr. Menendez would replace him. However, Jon Corzine came in out of nowhere and basically bought the seat. Steven stated that it was Menendez who decided to get more involved in local politics in Hudson County. He helped get Glenn Cunningham elected mayor of Jersey City, and it was Cunningham who was the first African-American mayor in the city. It was the mayor of Jersey City that always had been in a very powerful position, ever since the days of Frank Hague. Frank Hague was mayor from 1917 until 1947. He was an old-style machine politician; he strong-armed, threatened, blustered, and controlled. He was corrupt, and he also was efficient. Potholes were filled, snow was removed; the city worked. However, the friendship between Mr. Menendez and Mr. Cunningham fizzled out. Not long after, Steven was invited to City Hall so he could be honored with a proclamation acclaiming his war service. It was that proclamation that hangs outside his door that would change his life.

As a war veteran, Mr. Cunningham asked Steven many questions about his service, and about how he juggled it with his work on Wall Street. He asked Steven a lot of questions about the deployment, but he didn't think anything of it. At the same time, Steven was working on an M.B.A. from NYU and an M.P.A., a Master's in Public Administration, from Columbia. The work at his condo association took some time, he had a full-time job, and he still had a commitment to reserve duty. He did not have the spare time he was trying to fill; he did not have any spare time to breathe. About four months later, Steven hadn't spoken to the mayor since his proclamation, he received a phone call from the deputy mayor of Jersey City. He said that the mayor would like to talk to you.' Mr. Cunningham got on the phone and said, 'I'd like you to come in tomorrow. I have a few things I'd like to talk about.' At first, Steven remembered calling the mayor's office to complain about parking. He thanked the mayor, and he was surprised that he'd handle it himself, and so soon, but he didn't know what Steven was talking about. Mr. Cunningham urged Steven to come in the next day. He responded with an okay that he would after the markets closed.

Steven went into Mr. Cunningham's office, and they sat there with some of Cunningham's political supporters and assembly people, before starting to talk about getting involved in politics when you're young, in your 20s. Sometimes you lose before you can win, Cunningham told Steven, no matter what you're running for. Steven was 26 years old at the time and he had no idea what Mr. Cunningham was talking about, but he started talking about his sour relationship with Mr. Menendez. As it turned out, Mr. Menendez planned on running a full slate of officially approved candidates for local offices, and Mr. Cunningham wanted a slate to oppose it.

Even when Steven realized that he was being asked to run, he assumed, logically enough, that he was being solicited for a council seat, low on the slate. Mr. Cunningham told Steven that it wouldn't be a winning proposal, but that he would help him run for Congress. The more that Steven thought about it, the more he was intrigued. He discussed it with his family and friends, and on Monday Steven called back and gave Mr. Cunningham, 'OK, I'll do it.'" That's when Steven, with many of his friends, and his family began an old-fashioned, active campaign, meeting people, making connections, ringing doorbells, shaking hands, and working hard. He didn't know anything about campaigning at the time and didn't know how it worked. However, during Steven's run for Congress, he grew close to Mr. Cunningham, as they strategized together, but one day, about two weeks before the election. Then one day, Mr. Cunningham left Steven at 9 o'clock, and by 9:30 he had a massive heart attack. He died the following week.

Steven had lost the election resoundingly, but he did not lose his interest in politics. He realized that he liked meeting people, and he liked the whole process of running. Mr. Cunningham was replaced by Jerramiah Healy, who won both a special election and then a regular one. Steven ran for City Council off the party line. That is a notoriously difficult way to win a seat, particularly in a city as machine-ruled as Jersey City was then, but he did it. He began to understand more about politics. Steven and his team became focused on constituent services and slowly built a constituent base.

In 2012, Mr. Healy ran again. Inside the city, the incumbent was the head of a strong organization dedicated to keeping him in power and the organization in control, but outside he was a laughingstock. Mr. Healy had been photographed lying drunk on a porch; he came up with odd explanations about being overcome by young Hispanic women. The FBI visited him the day before a raid that culminated in 44 arrests for corruption. In general, he appears to have been Jersey City's own homegrown Rob Ford; he seems to represent the decadent, played-out last gasp of the party machine. The political machine of Jersey City may have lasted as long as it did at least in part because New Jersey lacks its own media, it has newspapers, but there aren't any large broadcasts that focus on local issues. Instead, it has to be a large-scale news story for it to break onto the news from New York or Philadelphia. However, Mr. Healy was seen as an institutional candidate and he was supported by prominent

Democrats, including President Obama, Senator Lautenberg, and Mayor Cory Booker of Newark, and by New York City's party-less but powerful Mayor Michael Bloomberg. The ads ran on television. Steven had been up in the polls, but his numbers plummeted. Yet, he still won. Running on a volunteer race, it took Steven years to build the support where he was running with small donors and Mr. Healy had big donors. Although, Steven ran a better campaign and won in every community.

Down the street from City Hall, a shul whose cornerstone reads 1920 stands padlocked and shuttered. It had been a mosque, but it seems abandoned now. In the blocks all around it, small businesses bustle; it is lively but does not look gentrified.

City Hall stands as an imposing structure, and showed its years, having begun in 1894, when it was finished two years later. It was not particularly well maintained in the years since Steven took office. Its high ceilings, marble floors, arched ceilings, spiral staircases, extensive woodwork, and painted detail. Its offices have pebbled windows that evoke images of black-and-white movies. The transoms high above them are not glass, as they must have been years ago, but painted plywood. The city clearly has transitioned for the better, and Steven gives both city hall and the city a kind of energy and charm that has moved the city to greater heights.

Being mayor of such as diverse community hasn't been easy for him. It has learned that its diversity is also one of the greatest assets, but also it is one of the greatest challenges. Jersey City is the only growing urban area in the state; its school district is growing quickly, but at the same time, other parts of the city felt as if they are being displaced or left behind. That has all changed since Steven has taken office. Every area of the city is being perfected with each year, each month, and each day that he has been in office.

Listening has been key for Steven and there is wisdom in this thinking, but at the same time, he has accomplished impressive changes for the city, including refurbishing the landmarked Loew's Theatre, a movie palace fallen on hard times, as well funding pre-kindergarten classes. It's challenging to be Mayor of Jersey City, where trust is fragile. In politics, a person can do the right thing 99 percent of the time, but it's the other one percent that people remember. Still, Steven brings excitement with him and every day is entirely different from the day before. With a determination to do good Steven has been able to mobilize and energize people who all believe, as he does, that you can make a change if you work for it with values, dedication, and passion. Within this story, a discussion of how the impact of being a political reformer to developing a solemn vow to serve the people is necessary to recreate community. It can be done, and it can be done outside of the political machines that many voters have become accustomed to believing that this is how government, in particular, politics is run. Very few will get past the trap of being confined to party expectations. However, within this story, we see how mayors such as Steven Fulop have been able to get passed this stigma, and have adopted a public office way of working that maintains a no strings attached way of working in government.

Chapter Two: A Case Study for Reform

The fact that political ideologies are tangible realities is not proof
of their vitally necessary character. The bubonic plague was an
extraordinarily powerful social reality, but no one would have
regarded it as vitally necessary.

— Wilhelm Reich

Just across from the Hudson River, the New York City
skyline has become the backdrop for the second largest to
Newark, and perhaps will soon become the largest city in
New Jersey. Jersey City has the charm of the Waterfront;
along with the bleakness of crime that infects many city
areas. It has become home to one of the most diverse
populations in the nation. Its history for being the first
permanent European community in the state for fur
trappers, farmers, and Dutch investors left their homes in
Amsterdam to set their sights on the west bank of the Deep
in the 1630s. An expansion of the railroads along the
waterfront, growing industrialization, and a steady supply
of workers to man the factories and run the trains continued
through the Civil War. By 1870, Jersey City's population
and economy had so outpaced its neighbors that the citizens
voted to merge into one larger city. However, following
World War II, many who had moved to Jersey City would

set their sights on the suburbs, and by the 1960s and the 1970s the city's economic state would decline. Even with the major recreational facility with breathtaking views, Jersey City had changed. Politics would soon become a prominent role for the city.

One of the famous and notorious mayors of Jersey City would take control of the city for the next thirty years. Frank Hague served seven consecutive terms and half of an eighth term in office from 1917 to 1947. The Hague era as it was known, spanned through the Depression and World War II. A masterful politician, his stronghold as 'the boss' took him beyond Jersey City, but into the state and a nation; his notoriety went far beyond what many in American politics looked to achieve.

Testing his popularity with voters, he worked behind the scenes, and managing to reorganize the Democratic Party in Hudson County was his political advantage to Jersey City. By dividing Jersey City into wards and smaller districts, neighborhood male and female leaders, dispensed patronage in return for votes. Hague's machine perfected the often-used political tactics of canvassing, transporting voters to the polls, and telephoning potential voters. Having gained the working class vote, a high-esteem filtered through the city. Hague kept the big business in check, especially the local railroads and utility corporations. At the same time, he stood in the way of labor unionism as synonymous with communism and anti-Americanism. A blend of violence and benevolence became Hague's legacy.

Frank Hague impressed an early benefactor and tavern owner Nat Kenny, the father of future nemesis Hague; along with constituents, he was able to capture his first political victory in 1896 as a ward constable. Political popularity and success continued for Hague, he was appointed a deputy sheriff in 1898, precinct leader in 1901, and ward leader in 1906, even with opposition to the decision being made by Democrat 'boss' Robert Little Nicky" Davis, the then mayor H. Otto Wittpenn, in 1908 Hague was appointed as custodian of City Hall. In 1911, Davis died and at that moment, Hague saw his chance to take on the role of the political boss after being elected street and water commissioner. Soon after, Hague then broke up with Mayor Wittpenn to join with other progressive reformers. Noting the rise to power of New Jersey's progressive reform Governor Woodrow Wilson, Hague championed charter reform for municipalities that would replace the mayor-council form of government with a commission form of government.

In 1916, under the Walsh Act, Hague would become commissioner of public safety over the fire and police departments. It allowed him to control appointments to these two vital service areas and thereby build a base for a patronage system that marked his political career. After decades of neglect, Hague imposed a strict code of conduct on the members of the police force in pursuit of his goal to lower the crime rate. During his mayoralty, the city was said to be "crime-free" with stepped-up security of one law enforcement officer for every three thousand residents and a cadre of plainclothes officers, recruited from the horseshoe, known as "Zeppelins." They were invaluable to Hague's hard-fisted brand of law and order.

By the end of the twentieth century, the role of political leadership would change through ethnicity and religion, with Irish Catholics controlling the majority of voters in the city. Hague became symbolic of the change they needed, after having the majority once held by Republican Protestants in earlier years. In the 1917 mayoral election, Hague outmaneuvered both Wittpenn and Republican Mark M. Fagan, the first elected mayor under the new city charter, and it was then that Hague would run with A. Harry Moore on the Democratic Party slate using the campaign slogan "The Unbossed." Moore ran slightly ahead of Hague--19,883 to 18,648--in the final count. But when the city commission met to organize for the new administration, they ignored the tradition that the man with the most votes had the first call on the mayor's job, Hague was unanimously elected mayor. However, once in office, Hague tried to exercise his power in the selection of governor. Democrats won six of the nine contests. Outside of the victories, Hague realized that to raise the tax valuation and obtain the much-needed revenue for the city, he needed to place a cooperative governor in the state house to appoint new members to the tax board. The candidate would be Hudson County Senator Edward I. Edwards. As Hague delivered on providing the votes for Edwards, Hague would be allowed to name some members of the public utilities commission and members of the Hudson County tax board and board of elections.

By the late 1920s, Hague identified with prohibition and supported another candidate who had the same opposition toward it, Alfred E. Smith for New York Governor, such support led Hague to become vice chair of the Democratic National Committee. As Smith lost his bid at the convention to become the party's presidential candidate, Hague quickly defected and cast his future with the party's choice, Franklin Delano Roosevelt (FDR). As if to make amends with the Roosevelt camp, Hague offered to stage a rally for Roosevelt in Sea Girt, New Jersey. It was the summer mansion of New Jersey governors. Hague had staged a rally for Smith at Sea Girt in 1928 and would hold one in 1939 for New Jersey gubernatorial candidate Charles Edison, whom he grudgingly supported to please Roosevelt. More than 120,000 Essex and Hudson County supporters of Roosevelt came to the governor's mansion. Hague proved himself a master politician. He could "get out the vote" by using strategies such as canvassing, providing transportation, and other incentives on Election Day. These tactics allowed Hague to deliver a plurality of votes to Democratic candidates of his choice in local, state, and national elections and became part of the Hague era. However, there was much more to Hague, the misuse of a list of registered voters.

One study claims that in 1937 Jersey City had 147,000 residents over age twenty-one, the legal voting age at the time while there were 160,050 residents registered to vote. The inflated voter registration numbers reportedly came from removing names from the list that had either passed away or moved away from the city under New Jersey's permanent voter registration law. When the state legislature to use electronic voting machines was introduced, Hague was said to have been responsible for getting Governor Moore to veto the legislation. However, such legislation was re-passed over his veto. Hague claimed that replacing the ballot box was unconstitutional, and with that, he was able to get the Hudson County Board of Freeholders to support his position.

Hague lived a lavish lifestyle that was unexplainable to the actual money being earned as mayor. Wealth didn't come from major corporation deals, but instead from real estate paybacks in the city, with a percentage from patronage and the city's gaming operations such as the numbers racket, card games, and off-track betting or "Horse Bourse." Hague would come to generate a three-percent salary kickback, known as "rice pudding," charged to the annual salaries of municipal employees and the mandatory thirty-percent return on salary raises. This allowed Hague to bring in between $500,000 to $1,000,000 a year. When the people of the city asked where the money was spent, Hague responded that the monies were used for "political purposes." This allowed Hague to tie in a bloated payroll of employees in city departments with questionable job descriptions and one of the best-paid police and fire departments, unfortunately, not an entirely new concept found in politics.

As Hague was more away from Jersey City vacationed in places such as Paris. He continued to oversee the state and county Democratic parties while continuing his role until 1949 as vice chair of the Democratic National Committee. In 1940, the city began to see a population decline. The loss of property owners and voters ultimately affected the city's revenue. Hague began to fail to represent in his administration new constituents and his popularity in the polls decreased. Returning veterans to the city began to react to machine-run politics and Hagueism became outdated. However, his last political stand was in building a New Jersey Constitution, such as Constitution would ensure a state income tax, a change regarding tenure and pensions of public employees, and taxation of church property.

After putting together a political rally for Harry S. Truman, thereafter, Hague left office and Jersey City due to the many pending lawsuits against him over salary kickbacks and his "cash" operations had long confounded federal and state investigations into his financial affairs. Hague also managed to avoid prosecution despite the many charges of corruption and impropriety. Many of his political tactics were not yet subject to the criminal code and possibly incriminating documents at City Hall were destroyed.

Since the days of Frank Hague, the idea of hard-hitting political machines continued to plague a city. A much-feared type of politician continued to emerge over the years. A successor to Hague, John V. Kenny, would control Jersey City and Hudson County Democratic politics for the next twenty years with equal acquisitiveness, but without luck. Kenny was convicted of federal charges that he was involved in a multi-million kickback scheme between city and county contracts. In 1971, Tom Whalen was convicted in the "Hudson Eight" federal net that swept up John Kenny. As the pattern of corruption continued, other Jersey City mayors would be convicted. Joseph "Newsboy" Moriarty was found guilty of playing the numbers game. Waging anywhere from twenty-five cents and up on any three-digit number, Moriarty made the game to be a secular ritual in Jersey City.

Outside of the city, Moriarty was unknown until a day in 1962 when workers pried open a car he'd stashed in a rented garage and discovered $2,590,525.20 in cash and more than three thousand dollars in bonds. Moriarty had forgotten to pay the garage rent through an oversight since he was already incarcerated at the time. He had banked his millions in lots of old cars in several rented garages around the city. News of the $2.5 million had made Moriarty become a national figure and furthered the city's reputation as an ATM for illegal cash in obscene amounts, while causing an increase in break-ins at rental garages across the city. The stories of illegal activity among politicians are not a new concept, with each of these men, now gone, the names that have plagued a city have been replaced with a new breed of politician.

On May 14, 2013, a new type of political reformer defeated an incumbent for the city's office for the election of City Mayor. With a reputation as a reformer during his tenure as councilman, he would over time turn back the hands of time, the corrupt ways that have made the second-largest city in New Jersey well-known. It would take much more than a well-thought-out election. Rather, it would take the commitment of ethical leadership. Not long after taking the oath, it was then, that a political reformer would start a new tradition within the City, one that would change the way the city would conduct business for real estate development bids and the everyday workings of City Hall. That tradition would become a movement for keeping an ethical code in government. Other ways for developing such movements was through reforming campaigns through a grassroots approach.

Chapter Three: The Political Reformer

Those who would give up essential Liberty, to purchase a little
temporary Safety, deserve neither Liberty nor Safety.

— Benjamin Franklin

We often hear about political issues, events, and news on
politicians both at the local, state, and national levels. One
of the principal reasons for it being everywhere is due to
the focus that is placed on it by media attention. What the
people hear on the news, the stories that are covered, and
how these stories are reported become crucial to
understanding how the people are governed. Many working
in politics recognize that people receive their information
through the media, this includes social media. However, it
was the early newspapers that had focused on political
ideologies or yellow journalism, where bold headlines were
used to entertain and appeal to a wider audience.

Politics is often a game of wits. However, the media has
found ways to taint a politician's reputation as being
unethical. With unreliable truths, he continued to hold to
maintaining an ethical principle, as the people learn about
case after case of corruption that may be built on
idiosyncratic standards of public corruption. This is where

the need for political reformers become a needed entity in politics. A political reformer holds the following criteria:

- According to Campaign for Political Reforms, political reform means improving the laws and constitutions to the expectations of the public. Requirements of all the segments of society are included in 'public expectations'. In a democracy, everybody bears equal rights of a single vote, but their equal participation in the decision-making process of the state is not ensured. Hence, political reform to ensure minimum economic equity is needed;
- Political reform means evolving such an electoral system by which gentility could be empowered in the state machinery; and
- Political reform means evolving such a constitution of a political party, so that the party working through that constitution may be able to work for political reforms.

Even still, sources such as the media still look for unbounded ways to hold politicians accountable for unethical behavior. This is something that I like to call the ham sandwich conviction, where any one of us, even a person who lives a simple life, could be found guilty of breaking some kind of law in their lifetime. However, when there isn't much negative behavior to find in a person, especially one serving in public office, it's the media's way of trying to build a case of wrongdoing. Instead, the media did whatever possible to plaque a politician's image to bring people to believe that they could be just as corrupt as so many other politicians before them. Speculation that brings about untrue stories to be believed, is the downfall of working in public office.

Finding political reformers is slowly taking shape in government, but the price is higher. It is common to hear of the importance of politicians giving endorsements for others running for office. It becomes so personal, that they are courted by other politicians as a means for officials to give fair warning of the repercussions that could happen to them for not endorsing. There is a give-and-take methodology to holding public office. The message is simple: outlining a good relationship with another politician, especially one of higher office, becomes seen as beneficial for the endorser's future ambition. This isn't always true. Maintaining a "no strings attached" philosophy, a plan was executed to ignore such means the desired plan, where there are more answers than there are questions.

Chapter Four: Reforming a Candidate

A party of order or stability, and a party of progress or reform, are both necessary elements of a healthy state of political life.

— John Stuart

Building on a campaign slogan "Enough" had allowed for a campaign strategy to be put together that was not often seen or heard of in political elections, listening to people in the city and their ideas. The question was asked before a crowded City Hall room to give their idea of what the city was like as a whole. The purpose was to paint a picture of what the future of their communities should be like, a plan to be described in less than three minutes. It was not an easy task when so much disconnect existed for decades, but even with so much anger and even more complaints, somewhere in that crowded room, there was a sense of optimism. People have had "enough." It would be these words that would shape a campaign for political reformers. The emphasis on communities becomes more than just a government building, instead, it becomes about improving the people by improving education or decreasing crime, but instead, the emphasis was on building a city of hope.

Hope is what a driving force among voters becomes when electing candidates this is due to the hope that there would be even one person that could bring about the necessary changes desired. For too long, exaggerated truths and broken promises become a central theme in politics. Many of the words that occupy campaigns are forgotten words. This is what helped to shape the idea of political reform among candidates. Political reformers soon learn while on the campaign trail just how many people were willing to get involved in their neighborhoods.

From building youth programs to contributing ideas to help the communities that they hope to serve slogans such as "enough" mean more than a slogan, rather it was a new way of thinking about government. Taking the line from speeches such as Martin Luther King's "I Have a Dream" has helped reformers finally prevail in an election and reach the people, but there is still a cautious hope in campaigns. However, the same cautious hope that left people expecting the worst can also bring forth hope for the best. It's what leads people to maintain positive thinking. That maybe, just maybe, with another candidate they could find the Promised Land.

All the while, political reformers listen and take notes. For not a second had passed that there was an interruption. The only promise that is felt are those where they could make was that the ideas that were shared with them would be kept. They assure the people that new leadership would take to heart their ideas. It wasn't the people that were the issue in governing, but the lack of transparency and accountability. The idea of "Enough" rang firmly in the minds of the people. More importantly, the idea of a political reformer's campaign slogan would become much more than just words, it was a chance to build positive change, that same desire for change that would bring candidates to run for public office.

Looking back at past elections, areas such as socioeconomic status also affect elections. Often, political reformers don't win because of their age or appearance, but because of their ability to return well on elections issues through progress. Despite the criticism that may be received by candidates for living in wealthier areas, political reformers in particular, can understand the frustrations that others just like themselves carry with them. What many in politics neglect to give achievement is the fact that political reformers have won elections with virtually no establishment support. This was the greater of the differences when comparing some political reformers to every other elected official in public office. Being able to beat candidates that had the backing of high-ranking, powerful congressmen, is a grassroots way of thinking that take many reformers to new heights in the election process.

Often, people advised that running a campaign solely on a grassroots initiative was the wrong way to go. However, in their hearts, political reformers know that it is the right way to win elections. By practicing this initiative not only in theory but as a strategy. They keep to a Grassroots Campaign to build support for progressive candidates, parties and causes through engaging everyday people in political action, reformers can bring awareness for a type of campaigning that made past leaders such as Abraham Lincoln well-respected. With an emphasis on small-donor fundraising, the use of a grassroots campaign helped him to change how someone who may have been seen as the average person interacts effectively with a political party. The results allow for many candidates to be able to sign on thousands of new supporters and raise millions of dollars. More importantly, for everyday people to see they could impact the political process.

When looking at the research on grassroots campaigns, in 2008, Grassroots Campaigns advocated for candidates who were running for office and helped to recruit volunteers to elect Barack Obama and other

Democrats in battleground states. Many key organizations "have helped to organize 7,480 house parties where volunteers made 2.14 million calls and recruited over 90,000 volunteers for Obama in swing states. Additionally, grassroots campaigns have "helped to register over 230,000 new voters in 13 battleground states, which helped to win many states and turned North Carolina blue for the first time since Jimmy Carter's election in 1976. It is an inventive way of thinking that separates political reformers from the usual politician. This strategy for campaigning is enforced because reformers no longer think like a candidate, but instead as a businessman. It isn't a far stretch for political reformers to use the experiences that they have gained working in industries, such as corporate America, to recognize how winning votes would mean reaching the people. It was the idea of bringing forth a grassroots initiative to mobilize a progressive movement.

Going door to door, with platforms such as hiring more police officers or improving business development, are some of the ways to reach the people in elections. However, what makes political reformers different is their ability to bring in the votes among the majority vote in both forecasted needed projects and the lower and middle socioeconomic classes of voters. A campaign that features several tactical innovations, one being not to distribute campaign signs to supporters. Another way is to recruit workers from the non-profit sector. Throughout the campaign process, this is how political reformers can put together a marketing strategy. This is how candidates have learned to become reformed.

It is a grassroots marketing plan that was carried out in the community. Taking advertising to the potential customer through a variety of strategies, such as a campaign kept to a firm plan often very effective for businesses in all stages of development. Political reformers use a grassroots approach to campaigning much like a newly formed business. It benefits them by getting their name out and establishing themselves as a brand that would stay on the voter's minds. In theory, when branding -- or re-branding -- a business, grassroots marketing can quickly establish an image.

The idea of using grassroots marketing was to saturate the people with talk about their platform. To do this effectively, reformers have no choice but to keep their branding, and their name in front of people, and on their minds. The message that they often have to send out is needed to be updated often, and they do. If not, the candidate's name and platform become repetitive and eventually ignored. It is what is called good business.

It may seem easy, but the truth is that even though the efforts of using a grassroots campaign often will work to their advantage, there are still many among political parties that will be watching political reformers. However, political reformers don't start this process alone. They have help.

Chapter Five: Growing Need for Reform

Never confuse the stated purpose of legislation with what it
would accomplish. Most enactments will be ineffective or
counterproductive.

— Jon Roland, September 8, 2004

Political reformers sharpen their skills to get ahead in the competitive sport that is known as politics. Many may seem like unlikely candidates, but they believe in using a grassroots approach to winning the elections. Very few politicians today can show not only in their words but through action their passion for helping others in need. Political reformers can do just that. Over the years, reformers look for ways to give back to the community first. This is at times what is found to be different from non-reformer politicians. Granted, each plays some role in giving back, either by starting them or giving to them, the difference is that reformers are giving to make a community better. For the non-reformer, it becomes a win for money and endorsements.

The growing need for government reform through a transformation of the public sector. With the growing need for reforms in the economy, energy, climate change, food supplies, and natural resources, political reform is essential to decrease the effects of economic and social breakdowns that are hurting the people and increasing both unemployment and poverty within the nation. Many times, reforms fall short of meeting the needs of the people. With much of the public sector being untouched, a faster reform must take place. A whole-government reform, which includes politicians that share a reform philosophy, for "governments assume a broader, more significant role in response to the crisis, it becomes ever more important that they should be efficient and effective—otherwise, they would compound the severity of the problems. This crisis is the public sector's ultimate test. However, many non-reform politicians are facing a crisis when it comes to engaging with the people. This is outside of modern technology, such as social media to connect and to change any negative issues within their communities. This is when political reformers have a healthy effect on the government.

Political reformers become engaged with the people and soon become known for being a first responder to the people. It is unheard of, no one in politics can be this conscious of listening and building relationships with the people. However, this can be seen in the reformer. There is a solemn vow to keep to a no-strings-attached high moral standard that reformers live by daily. Non-reformers are no strangers to the heavy-hitting political machines that made the name Tammany Hall famous. Corrupt politicians, like Tammany, use the government as a tool to gain votes that would bring power. Not just power to win and to stay in control, but profit as well. It's why the term political machine is so well known to the people, the reputation to get lost in greed and corruption. Many non-reformers believe that they are the law. The only similarity found between corrupt politicians and reform politicians is their intentions to improve the lives of others and the increasing need to bring people to find the positive side to living. However, reformers take it a step above non-reformers in that they are putting it into practice to oppose the lasting legacy of corruption and replace it with strong ethics. These are the actions political reformers are known for, in the past, present, and future, replacing corruption with ethics. There's no comparison.

Political reformers can accomplish much in a short period. It's not just a matter of achieving goals. Instead, it becomes a way of life. This is a way of decreasing the political machines of government. Over the past few years, nonperformers' political power is beginning to erode. Political reformers can capitalize on the corruption that has tainted government leadership. Even on the campaign trail, political reformers are building on slogans such as "Enough" to symbolize the end of the unethical behavior that has plagued the people for decades. Although it isn't the slogan that has as much importance to an election for public office, but rather the philosophy of campaigning. Not since Abraham Lincoln, have the people been able to experience such reproach.

Starting the election process takes years to build important alliances with those already involved in government. Before building a grassroots campaign and the decision to run for key positions in politics, political reformers often pay their dues first by working in the private sector. It is because of corporate America that many reformers are led to run for public office. Returning to the case study of a political reformer, it was the use of life experience and charity work that provided insight into becoming a political reformer and using it to an advantage.

In 2003, a potential candidate, Steven Fulop, had just been recruited to run for public office. Having returned from Iraq, he caught the attention of the current mayor of his town. A reformer by nature, Steven was prepped to run against a senior U.S. senator, Thomas Gordon who was also the chair of the House Democratic caucus. Being the most senior Hispanic federal legislator in the country, and the state's most senior House member. The state's top U.S. senator, who had resigned in 2001 — had also run again and took the state's other seat in 2003 — most in politics assumed that a top U.S. Senator would replace him. However, a man by the name of Jonathan Smith came in out of nowhere and bought the seat. It was then that Thomas decided to get more involved in local politics in the County's political system. He helped get the mayor at that time elected. It was Steven's work in the military that brought him to be chosen out of a proclamation ceremony honoring him and his troops by then-Mayor and fellow Marine, who was the city's first African American mayor, who had much more interest than being intrigued by military stories.

Believing that it was the work that he was already doing on a neighborhood group, Steven believed that the mayor wanted to talk about local issues. Rather, the then-Mayor didn't have just an interest in his deployment experiences, but rather he had persuasion on his mind. Steven went into an office, and he sat there, it was him, the then-Mayor, and some of the mayor's political supporters and assembly people. This is how the then-Mayor started talking about getting involved in politics when you're young, in your 20s. Saying that sometimes you lose before you can win, no matter what you're running for. He had something bigger to discuss with Steven— a run for Congress against a political rival of the Mayor. This inevitably would start a new chapter for him.

Taking by bicycle to campaign, plunging into a congressional race against a powerful figure in the State's County and Washington, D.C., it was the Mayor that had worked with Steven in his campaign. On April 22, 2004, the Mayor posted a letter on a County politics message board with added support for Steven's work and service as a reformer:

"Good morning.

The State's second-largest city was without a Congressman.

For the last 14 years, the City has been carved up by the political bosses outside our borders.

We have seen our political currency diminished.

We have seen our needs put behind the interests of the outside political bosses.

It is time now for the City to send a strong voice for its needs to Washington.

In this culture dominated by corruption, and criminal investigations it is time for a fresh face to represent the City and the 13th Congressional District in Washington.

Marines remember Corps values.

These are the values we are guided by.

First and foremost, Marines never leave anyone behind.

Our present Congressman has left the City behind!

It's time to call out the Marines to fight for the City.

And Congressman Gordon was never a Marine, soldier, sailor, or airman.

Right now I'd like to introduce a man who has those Corps values and will use them to fight for the City and the entire 13th Congressional District.

Steven Fulop, a man who volunteered to fight for his Country and Democracy in Iraq,

He has returned from his tour of duty in Baghdad.

He is currently in the Marine Corps Reserves and now wants to serve his country in the Halls of Congress representing the City and the 13th District.

• Steven Fulop, 27-year-old City resident.

• Executive with Goldman Sachs.

• True patriot, gave up a great job at Goldman Sacks following the attacks on America, 9-11 to become a Marine in the U.S. Marine Reserves.

• Risked his life in Baghdad, Iraq for our country, and freedoms.

• continues to fight for his country, here as a congressional Candidate.

• But Thomas Gordon and the political bosses don't want to face a challenge, a new voice.

• They sent out their thugs to intimidate petition signers who support Mr. Fulop. That's not American, that's illegal.

Rev. ALLEN,

• A man of god who is a community activist and a spiritual leader in the City.

• Rev. Allen's heart is with the community, as he has shown and he will be a great advocate for the people of the City.

SEAN CONNORS

• The City's Police Officer who risks his life every day for the residents of our community.

• He will represent us well in Congress because his heart is with the community."

Although the names used were fictitious, Steven would suffer a greater setback than just losing the election when the then-Mayor had unexpectedly passed away in the run-run election. His greatest mentor, protector, and patron in politics were gone. Steven stated when asked about leaving the primary race for Congress. Suddenly, the Mayor passed away from a massive heart attack during a time when Steven was still campaigning, and he lost a very close friend and a mentor. As a neighborhood leader selected by the Mayor early in the spring to run in the primary, Steven's response was with great strength, they were staying in the race. In his mind, that's what the mayor would have wanted. Steven's thinking was that they were going to give the people of the Thirteenth District a choice. He realized that it would be an uphill battle. The irony of a mentor and friend that would lead Steven to one day that he too could hold the Mayor's position in the City.

It would have been seen as a major setback for Steven, but instead, it helped to align him with veteran County operatives who pledged to help him to run for council. Become the people's choice in City politics, he would go on to make a name for himself. Election after election, the true test would come in time. In a letter to the people of the City, Steven took to what has become the modern-day pen and paper, technology, to prepare for re-election for city council:

"I hope you all had a good weekend and I wanted to send you a quick note concerning the political landscape for next year's election in the City.

Since our upset victory in 2005, I hope you agree that we have accomplished some important objectives that we set out to achieve. In the last three years alone, our Council office has sponsored and passed more legislation to improve the City than any other Council office. This includes but is not limited to, establishing the strictest pay-to-play laws in the state, a lead poisoning policy that received statewide coverage, a security camera policy to improve safety throughout the City, and some of the strictest health sanitation policies in the state. Furthermore, while trying to improve responsiveness and professionalism, we have successfully advocated for financial responsibility and improved educational opportunities for our children.

With an election next year for the City Council and Mayor, I am honored that in such a short period that there has been so much support and interest for me to run for the Office of Mayor. Our team has grown to be a group of 230 community volunteers. Simply put, this was accomplished through a progressive representation of the community's best interests—not through the politics-of-old patronage system that I believe has been a virus inflicted upon our City in years past.

Similarly, in a short four months, our election fund has raised more campaign dollars than any sitting council member in the state. This accomplishment is not about me, however, but a belief amongst residents of the City that there is great untapped potential for us to achieve excellence in the City.

For me, politics has never been about status, titles, or public position, but about purpose. I believe that public service is important whether through a community group, in professional life, or in government. My view has never wavered regardless of the opportunities presented for bigger titles or positions. While humbled by an outpouring of support to run for higher office, I have decided to seek re-election in the community that has given me the opportunity and privilege of representing them on the Council. In knowing what my goals were when I set out into public service I think this is the right thing to do in being true to my initial core beliefs on the reasons I entered government, as well as my responsibilities to the people I have represented on completing properly the issues that I have started as a councilman.

I thank you again for the opportunity to serve in the greatest city I have known.

Semper Fidelis, Always Faithful.
Sincerely yours"

The philosophy to work with the people in his ward for the next seven years would bring many political reformers such as Steven Fulop to run for their next title. Running for public office is similar to each election, but the difference is the challenges that lie ahead in convincing the people that campaign promises will be kept. For many already involved in politics, it is a watch-and-see game. However, for many political reformers, elections are an opportunity to reach the people through areas such as their heritage, or their roots as a means to identify with voters, and for voters to identify with them. This is how some reformers use their experiences to reach the people, and ultimately win votes.

Chapter Six: Diminishing the Party

A grateful heart is the beginning of greatness. It is an expression of humility. It is a foundation for the development of such virtues as prayer, faith, courage, contentment, happiness, love, and well-being.

— James E. Faust

To best understand how political parties affect reform thinking. Looking into how parties were developed helps to understand the ideology of its movement. We see it begin in 1787 when a group of people began calling themselves the Federalists. This was the first United States political party. In 1796, anti-Federalists gathered around Jefferson. Members of Jefferson's group called themselves Democratic-Republicans. Political parties were not held favorable to many holding public office. The idea of being a part of a political party strongly comes out of a few ideas. Some of these ideas include ideology, policy position, and public acceptance, as history repeats itself.

Political parties have changed the landscape of how candidates run for election. Often built on the idea that to be successful and to hold office, one must be supported by either the Democratic or Republican party. Over the years since its establishment, political parties such as the Republican Party sharply are taking a path toward being diminished. The current state of the Republican Party is changing, with candidates slowly becoming split between conservatives and liberals. A similar situation that had occurred during the time of Abraham Lincoln, as the Whig Party would become a party made up of conservatives and liberals. The change in political views brought about the creation of the Republican Party.

The Orthodox Conservative ways that were a driving force in American public policy, have begun to make the Republican Party less popular among the people. Not since Dwight Eisenhower, has the Republican Party found a decrease in a candidate supporting the foundations such as free trade and supporting the value of military alliances. The idea of every man is created equal, is the source of every man's freedom and dignity. This was the idea of building the Republican Party more than a hundred years ago, and the reason why the nation was founded. When the foundations of God are decreased and an increased focus on transgender issues begins to exist, this is when the signs of destruction may be seen in the Republican Party. With few and fewer candidates supporting the foundations of conservatism the idea of government created by the people, for the people has less purpose. Instead, the conservative candidate diminishes, along with the formation of its party. This change in a candidate may be seen during the time of the presidency of Dwight Eisenhower.

It was a 1909 address that President Eisenhower gave, which stated that "the reader should bear in mind that the Republican Party was breaking up into conservative and liberal factions." As Roosevelt changed his position from Republican to Democratic, the decision was an important step, one that would determine his political standing for life. Choosing one party over another, the idea is to remain a life member of that party. It is a decision that may often lead to the diminishing of the Republican Party, one where over time, history may repeat itself, as the party struggles to maintain strength during elections. It was similar diminishes were found during the development of the Whig Party and its diminish toward becoming the Republican Party and its principal goal for stopping the expansion of slavery.

The Republican Party had a principal goal, that goal was to stop the expansion of slavery into the western territories. Abraham Lincoln, the sixteenth president of the United States, had been involved with the Whig Party, which was disintegrating due, in large part, to sectional rivalries. Since Lincoln was personally opposed to slavery, he found the Republican Party platform much to his liking. George Washington, the first president of the United States, had no desire to be a part of a political party and hoped that they would never be formed. Washington was strongly admired for his strong leadership qualities. Washington was unanimously elected president in the first two national elections. He oversaw the creation of a strong, well-financed national government that maintained neutrality in wars such as the French Revolutionary War. Washington suppressed the Whiskey Rebellion and won acceptance among Americans of all types. Washington's incumbency established many precedents, still in use today. This was completed without the support of Washington's participation in a political party and the development of its brand today.

Political parties carry an idea, a notion, and a brand that is presented to the voter that markets candidates and current elected officials, this is important when providing establishment support to political candidates in their quest for being elected. Brands are important since they provide information on the character and identity of products and companies. In this case, the product is the candidate. The loss of Republican candidates has been attributed to a fundamentally flawed candidate who has emerged into the primaries with a tarnished brand. The Republican Party has become popularized with negativity before a campaign has begun. The popularized negativity found among the Republican Party is strong enough, that it can no longer be able to sustain its most important product, a candidate. Branding, especially among political parties, becomes essential to the ability to bring the people to want to become a part of their vision and mission.

The subconscious mind is as powerful as a vote. For a candidate as part of a tarnished brand, the ability to impact decision-making through the ability to reach the people through the emotional and rational sides of an individual. It is essential to connect stories that maximize the subconscious mind to win an election. However, according to Turner, the Republican Party may consider using storytelling as a major pathway to rebranding the party.

Storytelling may be used in three paths, habits, beliefs, and stories, in the following ways:

- *Habits* are our routines in life. Neuroscience supports that habits become the autopilot for our decisions, which is why habits are so difficult to break. It also demonstrates why the habit of telling the same story becomes a major part of how we act and view our life;

- *Beliefs* are the conclusions we make by living life. It is important to understand that all beliefs are not equal. If we attach emotion to a belief, then that belief becomes more important to us. Often these beliefs are referred to as our core principles and values; and

- *Stories* impact beliefs because one of the components of a story is *emotion.* It is often the emotional impact of a story that has the most profound impact on the success of the story. Neuroscience supports why emotions play such a critical role in storytelling.

Brands are symbols that provide signals about the identity of a product. The ability of the Republican Party to reinvent its brand will be challenging. In a survey conducted of 1200 U.S. voters, using fourteen positive brand words and phrases, were to tell researchers which phrases were better to describe the party, Republican and Democrat. The Democrat Party ranked increasingly higher than the Republican Party in thirteen of the fourteen phrases.

Several key areas, including: "offering hope of a vision for the future," "cares about people like me," "clearly explains how its actions will benefit me," "understands issues facing the middle class," "works to bring about change," "honest and ethical" and "smart and innovative" Other keywords, such as: hopeful, caring, beneficial, understanding, changing, ethical, and innovative had a high correlation or relationship as brand signals of the Democratic Party. The brand signals found to have a strong relationship to the Democratic Party would align with important factors that attribute to a favorable view of Nike and its ability to have the most appealing colors, in turn being the least important factor for buying athletic shoes.

The Republican Party may have a significant brand issue. It is essential to correct it through immediate action, which may mean the party's brand and image are necessary for recovery. For any brand that has lost a positive image, clearly establishing what the party stands for may mean relating to the concerns that matter deeply to the consumer, while differentiating itself from the Democratic Party. Communicating the differences in a way that is simple and easy to understand, but more importantly, introducing a leader who reflects on core values, as well as addressing the emotional and rational side, habits, beliefs, and emotions, may be needed to rebuild the Republican Party brand and its diminish.

More and more, we see that politics and its elections are being driven by party lines. This is what I like to call red versus blue. Many involved as political reformers will take a side, however, will easily switch from the red to the blue and vice versa. The loyalty isn't to a political party. That's not the solemn vow, but instead, the oath is believed to be of the people. To understand where the red and blue came from, the history of these colors is of great interest to understanding why political reformers will keep loyalty to a political party and its color at bay.

Chapter Seven: Social Media Transparency

Smartphones and social media expand our universe. We can connect with others or collect information easier and faster than ever.

— Daniel Goleman

The use of media such as newspapers, opinion columns, and blogs; for many politicians may often bring fear. This fear is brought on because of a loss of power to control what is being said about the many men and women who hold public office. However, just as easily as a media source could be hurtful to a politician, it can also help them. This is especially true during elections where attaining endorsements may be seen as crucial. Even with this thinking, there has yet to be evidence to show that the use of newspapers has made a difference in how people vote. With as much publicity being used between social and print, sources such as newspapers can't control their readers. Although with the decline in newspapers fast approaching and social media replacing much of how people receive information, there have been several politicians who are taking to their cell phones and computers. Political reformers have become one of those politicians.

After taking office, many in politics, including reformers, are using social media to communicate directly with the people. The use of social media can also increase transparency. Transparency has been a key goal for candidates when running for public office and for many people, the ability to use social media has been a 'breath of fresh air.' It's unheard of for a politician to be attainable to the people. However, not only does the use of social media increase communication and transparency, but it also increases credibility. Using social media presence as a public forum for the people has led politicians to have more direct contact with the city and its people. Instantly, politicians can get their message out without filters and can relay exactly what he wants to say without it being altered. Facebook and Twitter a natural among politicians at all levels of government.

A report issued by the Congressional Research Service concluded that members of Congress are rapidly and avidly taking to forms of social media that did not exist fifteen years ago. The advantages for each are the distribution of immediate speed at a minimal cost. Back in 2010, surveys had shown 205 of five hundred thirty-eight members of Congress on Twitter accounts and three hundred and forty-nine on Facebook with the numbers growing. Among members of Congress, one study noted usage varied greatly. During a two-month study, sixteen congressmen tweeted at least one hundred times in sixty days, including one who alone was approximately two hundred and ninety tweets.

Facebook was great for organizing supporters, for events; while he used Twitter to specialize in getting messages to supporters very quickly. Traditional means were still important to him. Using interviews with the press and public appearances allowed the people to be there without physically being in the room. It was a unique way of connecting. Politicians, both reformers and non-reformers, are making appearances across the nation and can keep up with the momentum of delivering information to the people through social media. It also allowed for it to be a voice for the people.

With a business approach, politicians can use the strength of their followers to build new ones. The use of social media affords the spread of the message much further. Politicians can make announcements and connect the people to articles in the newspaper that directly affected them and the city's future while improving public service.

Using social media to reconnect with the city and to learn more about what they wanted, politicians, especially reformers, can listen to their constituency's problems more directly. They can show their supporters exactly what they and what the government is doing to help. One example has been over the winter months. Using the quote: "There isn't such thing as bad weather, only different types of good weather" -John Ruskin. Nevertheless, we are plowing!" Political reformers can drive the message to all that treating the streets was being accomplished.

Political reformers are using social media in much the same way businesses do: by 'trying to convince the public to embrace something.' In this sense, reformers can provide a public perception by broadcasting both positive and some not-so-positive information via social media outlets.

One way to communicate transparency, while increasing credibility has been through writing. Writing on topics such as endorsements, the economy, health care coverage, veterans, gun reform, and current issues that have directly affected the people. Political reformers are building a different type of platform outside of the political arena. Instead, their focus has been on bringing awareness by using a perspective that many do not have a chance to learn about through their own local and state politicians.

In other ways, political reformers are continuing to brand the city through writing monthly opinion blogs. Much of what is expressed, while bringing forth insight into what has impacted lives. In one politician's blog, "Honoring Dr. King's Legacy To Leave No One Behind," a reformer used the history of Dr. Martin Luther King not only to provide readers with a greater understanding of Dr. King's goal to bring people together, but he also provided the progress that is occurring in the City.

> "This enduring image of Dr. King in the City -- the diversity of his audience -- is prevalent in our own time nearly 50 years after his assassination. Certainly, great progress has been made but his vision for America has not yet been fully achieved. Too many Americans have not had a real opportunity to succeed, and turning a blind eye to their plight is not a policy, it's a dereliction of responsibility for all of us as citizens. In the City, we take that responsibility seriously.
>
> Last year, we opened a prisoner re-entry center that is the first of its kind in the State and serves as a national model for reintegration by coordinating all the necessary services for this diverse population. We have coordinated and streamlined a myriad of

reintegration tools to provide clients with addiction treatment, sober housing, and employment training. The center assists the unemployed and ex-offenders with addiction recovery, and transitional housing, as well as job training and employment. It is a home of second chances, which will assist people in living productive lives through faith, recovery, and work.

To date, we are encouraged by the results and hope they will be replicated in city after city. In the Marines, we are taught never to leave a man behind. Dr. Martin Luther King believed similarly. As we celebrate his life and achievements today -- and every day -- it is our responsibility as Americans to leave no one behind. That's the best way to honor Dr. King."

Other issues that face the government can be expressed through social media. In a post on the effects of crime, an opinion was expressed not only for his City but for many cities in the nation, as he wrote about the importance of policing in his post.

"Crime recognizes few boundaries - urban or suburban. That's why it's so important to have police departments cooperate as regional crime fighters, especially to slow the movement of guns and drugs. But fighting crime is more than just good police work. We also need to remedy some of the problems that cause crime to occur by focusing not only on public safety but job creation, housing security, and recreation opportunities as well."

Driving the important point of fighting crime can be achieved by collaborating efforts and resources between cities by building a model of prevention. He continued to outline such a model for the people through a means of collaboration.

> "Examples of how our three cities will collaborate on public safety matters include sharing information, tracking criminals who travel from city to city, trading gang intelligence, and offering communal police manpower and task forces, as well working together on programs such as Cease Fire and departmental efforts for minority recruiting. At the same time, the cities will jointly agree to issue municipal Requests for Proposals that call for bidders to subscribe to responsible gun sales and use, as the City has already done with positive results. In addition, we are partnering with University Policing to help guide our efforts."

Building further on transparency and increasing credibility to the people, he went on to write:

> "This is just the beginning of a more in-depth conversation about how to enhance and engage our communities, work together, and develop strong partnerships to benefit our residents. No doubt, there is more we can and will do moving forward. Still, as

a first step, we are moving from hope to action. This is a path other city governments should follow."

With each method of communication, this politician used not only social media to instill confidence within his community, but he also used his writing on blogs to increase his presence to the people. Even as he began his career as mayor he not only chose to provide professionalism but also expressed his thoughts as to the challenges that were ahead of head.

In another post, Endorsements Hardly Matter, a political reformer discussed how endorsements should be used when they will improve the lives of their constituents; along with how the idea of endorsements being the 'Holy Grail of campaign momentum' have ultimately become a thing of the past. This way of communicating to the people a view that can be respected. It shows that the decisions being able to are being considered first before acting upon them. Something at times politicians neglect to achieve.

> "As the new mayor of a city, I couldn't be more excited about the challenges ahead. From a political standpoint, people often look at me curiously because of my younger age while being responsible for a city the size of ours; however, I think I've learned a fair amount through the years.

My predecessors have included a colorful array of chief executives; perhaps the most notable of who appears regularly on HBO's *Boardwalk Empire* and once summarily declared "I am the law." And he meant it. During those times, the endorsements by city mayors of their candidates of choice often made the difference in local and state and often national elections. Quite literally, they could choose the winner of many elections because of their iron-fisted control of both the party apparatus and the voters who depended on the party for jobs and support.

Times have changed. Not just in my city, but across the nation. That's a good thing.

Running for office means communicating the power of your ideas and letting voters know how your experiences relate to their lives. My background is a little unusual. I quit a lucrative career in finance to join the Marines as an enlisted man and served in Iraq after 9/11 because of my love for my country. Once I finished my tour of duty, I decided there was far more I could do to change the City for the better in government than in the private sector. I bucked party elders, campaigned hard about my vision for one of America's most diversely populated cities, and have beaten incumbents two times.

Of course, I also lost an election -- badly -- along the way which taught me that passion and a resume by themselves won't do it. Electoral success comes from connecting with voters and giving them the confidence that candidates can deliver on their ideas."

As a political reformer, being active in using social media became a winning strategy for many holding public office, this is especially true during an election year. Although veteran politicians are beginning to become accustomed to the use of Twitter and Facebook, what political reformers can accomplish outweighs the years before working campaigns. Indeed, social media can be a powerful tool for modern politicians. Connecting with voters on an individual basis is so important, and with social networking sites, a politician doesn't have to organize a door-to-door neighborhood campaign to achieve that connection.

Chapter Eight: Developing a Community

A healthy social life is found only when, in the mirror of each soul, the whole community finds its reflection, and when, in the whole community, the virtue of each one is living.

—Rudolph Steiner

Beginning a public office term as a newly appointed or re-elected official begins by generating a sense of renewal and hope for the people and the area that they live in. A buzz of the work that is to create change, but also for betterment is anticipated. This is especially true in those beginning months of the new term in office. However, since 1980, the hope for the better solely became relevant, as real estate developers, mostly coming from large cities are at times diminished. Instead, many areas, such as cities, are left with abandoned factories and warehouses that have taken over their landscape. Many cities have been home to thriving companies such as Colgate and Emerson Radio, however after World War II, many of the jobs and people who worked in these companies have left the cities to pursue living in the suburbs. Some political reformers understand this reality and the reason why their cities had been taking a decline.

The real estate boom of the 1980s had at one time brought high-rise condors and shopping centers. The waterfront became one of the premiere addresses for well-known companies, Goldman Sachs and J.P. Morgan, companies that opted to be adjacent to the downtown area. Such companies nurtured revenue for the city. While this type of development broadened the city's tax base, it also divided many lifelong residents. A separation between immigrants that lived in the city and newly-residing professionals brought about what was known as "the tale of two cities."

The growing demand for luxury condo development s made a difficult impact on the city for quite some time. It doesn't take long for political reformers to realize this reality. The reality is that in cities, where more than fifty-two percent of the families, that they are serving, speak a language other than English at home. Other concerns such as the socioeconomic state of families also impacted reformers and governing as a whole. With more than sixteen percent living below the poverty line, political reformers look for ways to connect the various ethnic and socioeconomic groups of their communities. We see this within both large and smaller cities. In the case of one mayor, within two weeks of starting his role in public office, during Ramadan, a young man who was being chased by a gunman ran into a mosque filled with worshippers. Sending off a façade of bullets within the mosque, panic instantly came over those that filled their house of worship. The next day, this mayor showed up at the mosque alongside the police chief. His promise was protection. These were words never heard before within the city. His promise rang through. For the rest of the holy month, an increase in police presence around the mosque. It was just another reason to believe.

Thinking of more fortified ways to improve the city, he believed the one way to achieve this was to move real estate development away from the pricey area of the Waterfront and instead into building among the inner-city districts. With that goal in mind, he established incentives for builders through a thirty-year tax abatement policy, which included a good-faith clause requiring any developer or business receiving breaks to hire people within the City to be workers and apprentices. By putting such a policy in place, in the last year and a half, real estate development has skyrocketed.

Kushner Real Estate Group, a real estate developer, along with Trump KBR, would soon build partnerships to take over projects in the Waterfront neighborhood of the

City. New buildings such as Trump Bay Tower and a three-tier development project, a 2.4 million-square-foot development to be completed by KRE Group, have become focused on the City, as an increase in development, not just as a means increase to revenue. Bringing in developers with the proposed tax abatement policy allows for jobs to be created, with one project estimating to create between four and five hundred union construction jobs.

With well sought-out developers such as Kushner Real Estate Group, have already begun to break ground within the city with a 660 million dollar project which includes three residential towers, other developers soon followed. The main downtown area once known for having a thriving commercial business of retail stores and theaters; along with continuing to be the transportation center was deteriorating, and what was once recognized by its thriving scenery began to be substituted with empty stores and lots.

As time moved forward, the people became tired of progress not being made to their neighborhoods, working with Kushner, who had pledged millions for infrastructure upgrades and a renovation of the landmark Loew's Theater, jumpstarted improving the city. Although the mayor had been faced with some disapproval for his tax abatement policy, nonetheless, it would be worth the investment. An example was the restoration of the city's theater. Bringing in up to $15 million for such a project could bring him to becoming a hero for the city. In reality, building a jewel as impressive as the Loew's Theater could never happen today, it would in the end cost much more than the projected amount that it would take to restore.

For the mayor, the development of a new project brought about an exciting day because it would become a real game-changer for his City in so many ways. Projects were going to change the City, and it would certainly change the downtown area as well. It would then literally transform and recreate the entire City skyline. For a mayor, but also a businessman, that would be no small accomplishment, it would be nothing short of something that the entire City and its people would be proud of, and nothing more significant for positive change.

With the City becoming a community built on harmony, it is also a community of people that is peacefully welcoming immigrants from every nation. He devised over the past four years as mayor the mission of 'One City,' where every resident has the opportunity to build a safe and happy home for themselves and their families. Both he and his administration continue to work hard to prove that the best things about their city do not start and stop at the waterfront. Regardless of ethnicity, gender, sexual orientation, religion, or income, the thinking behind 'One City,' is for every resident to have the ability to live a healthy, productive life in the City.

The City is now considered to be a national model for police diversity. As a result, nearly 70% of the new officers hired since 2013 have been minorities, they have become a City that welcomes people from all backgrounds and walks of life.

Since taking office, he has continued to develop the City, with over 3,500 jobs being added. This allowed for the opening of over 300 new small businesses, and reduced unemployment to a 25-year low of 4.1%, all within the last year alone. In 2015, the City had nearly 7,000 residential units under construction – more than anywhere else in the state and a record for the City itself, while creating affordable housing units across the entire city. This was the most affordable housing unit created in the last two years as in the last 8 years combined, along with constructing the first veteran housing project.

Using his financial skills, he brought about further changes, such as thinking fully of the working class. Pushing through a paid sick leave ordinance that would require businesses with ten or more employees to give their workers one hour of sick time for every thirty hours of work, he had called such measures a 'human dignity issue,' by continuing to believe in the people, he believed that the people shouldn't have to risk losing a job or a day's worth of wages. It was one of many causes that he initiated that would become an example for other local governments statewide. This was all done by keeping to his solemn vow, as he brought about the needed changes to rebuild a City. This was unheard of, especially during a time when politics has become rampant with corruption.

This is one of many examples of how political reformers have been able to change governing and its communities. By using business skills, many reformers can put their skills to use for those living, working, and visiting within their communities. This is often the thinking behind political reformers. The idea is to reinvest in the community by using people who live there daily. It re-establishes to some extent a level of ownership and pride back to the community's streets.

Part II

Chapter Nine: Truth Behind Lying in Politics

If politics is like show business, then the idea is not to pursue excellence, clarity, or honesty but to appear as if you are, which is another matter altogether.

— Neil Postman

We watch with fascination as candidates for the world's most powerful candidates potentially speak falsehoods and allegations of dishonesty. It's a challenge to know if a politician is lying. Many of us have given little thought to our lies and to how they compare with politicians' deceits.

For more than two decades, researchers of different stripes have examined humanity's less-than-truthful underbelly. This is what they have found: We all stretch the truth. We learned to deceive as toddlers. We rationalize the fabrications that benefit us. We tell little white lies daily that make others feel good.

Now magnify that to how politicians may distort the truth more often, use more self-justifications, and deceive in larger ways, and with more consequences, experts in psychology and political science.

There is more worry about lying in public life. This is especially true for politicians than ever before. When lies succeed, they make it more tempting to lie. Lies can stick. They can have a lingering effect, even if they are debunked, and deception starts early.

Children learn to lie at an average of about 3 years old, often when they realize that other people don't know what they are thinking.

There is extensive research on children and lying. Lee set up an experiment in a video-monitored room and would tell children there was they can have that's behind them, but they can only get it if they don't peek. Then the adult is called out of the room, returns a minute later and asks if they peeked.

At age 2, only 30 percent lie. At age 3, half do. By 5 or 6, 90 percent of the kids lie and Lee said he worries about the 10 percent who don't lie. We explicitly teach our kids to tell white lies, with parental coaching about things like saying how much they love gifts from grandma, and it's a lesson most of them only get around age 6 or older. In 1996, DePaulo, author of "The How's and Whys of Lies," put recorders on students for a week and found they lied, on average, in every third conversation of 10 minutes or more. For adults, it was once every five conversations.

A few years later, Robert Feldman at the University of Massachusetts taped students in conversations with total strangers and got similar results with the participants not realizing they were lying until they watched themselves. We lie constantly. The problem is there are many shades of truth-bending. Experts split on whether to count white lies and "social lubrication" that makes civilized operate. When your spouse tells you that you don't look fat in that outfit when you do, does it really do any harm?

There's a difference between white lies and real lies. Some lies fall under politeness norms and are not very harmful. Other lies are self-interested and those are the harmful ones. Those are the ones that harm relationships, harm trust. However, others see no distinction: It doesn't matter if the attempt was motivated by good intentions and it doesn't matter if the lie is about something little. Regardless, society rewards people for white lies.

We're trained to be deceptive Feldman said. "If we're not, if we're totally truthful all the time that's not a good thing, there's a price to be paid for that. We don't like people who tell us the truth all the time. From there it's only a small leap to what politicians do.

The lies that we accept from politicians right now are lies that are seen as acceptable because it's what we want to hear, such as a spouse saying that an outfit flatters you. Or perhaps we feel that lying is necessary.

People want their politicians to lie to them. The reason that people want their politicians to lie them is that people care about politics. Washington is a dirty place and that lying is very helpful to get your policies implemented.

When people deceive beyond white lies, they spend a lot of effort justifying and rationalizing what they are doing. They engage in something we call justified dishonesty. It happens when people's desire to be ethical clashes with the desire to profit or get something. In that case people are willing to lie just a bit just long as it seems legitimate ad with a rationale to lie. There is the thinking that it's okay and rationalizing that there is a meaningful purpose. Politicians convince themselves that the ends justify the means and the reasons they are doing it.

Dishonesty is contagious. Although most people want to be honest. The public tends to believe things – even if they are false – that confirms what we already believe" and come from news sources and partisans that they already trust and agree with, however, politicians should be held up to a higher standard. Over the decades, they and the government have been more deceitful and unwilling to tell the public something that could hurt them politically. When

President Dwight Eisenhower misled the public about a spy plane captured by the Soviet Union, lying was the exception. By the time President Bill Clinton strained the meaning of the word "is" testifying before a grand jury, it was more common. In Washington, deception is the gift that keeps on giving. However, there's a high cost in everyday society – a loss of trust that is difficult to regain – when someone is discovered to be lying. There are also costs to the liar. The effect of deception on the body and brain and how much energy it takes to create and maintain a lie causes stress. The Marines share a belief and practice system that works.

Semper Fi is the Marine Corps motto which means "Always Faithful." This phrase encompasses the Marines' dedication to their country, their fellow Marines, and their families. Marines are expected to live up to this motto both in and uniform. Although it may not be a public office, Marines take on the public trust, similar to politicians to protect and to serve.

Chapter Ten: What is an Oath?

The decision that has to be made was whether it was material, whether he knew he was lying under oath, and whether he did it willfully. I think that's required of any prosecutor who is charged with an investigation of this.

— Barbara Olson

An oath is defined as an oath as a ritual act, or more specifically a "speech act." It is an oath that includes one kind of speech act. Taking an oath expresses a specific intention to others, using words like "I promise to" or "I swear that." The intention when taking an oath is not limited to the moment someone articulates the words of the oath. Oath-taking is also about the intention in the future to commit to acting a certain way. One example is the vows taken by couples during their wedding in front of witnesses. British philosopher John L. Austin called oaths "performative utterances."

The engaged couple, for example, declares to marry each other by speaking their vows to one another. They make a deliberate choice of their own free will. However, it was the Roman soldiers who first gave their allegiance. The ritual of taking oaths goes back centuries in Western Europe. In antiquity, oaths were often demanded of religious and governmental leaders, as well as those in certain professions. In ancient Rome, oaths were also demanded of soldiers.

The most solemn military oath – directly invoking the Roman gods – was the "sacramental." By this oath, soldiers swore allegiance to their specific general or commanding consul and, later, to the emperor. Disobedience could earn severe punishments.

A tapestry scene showing swearing oath on holy relics to William, Duke of Normandy. Myrabella via Wikimedia Commons

On some occasions, oath-breaking was tested by resorting to divine intervention. The virgin goddess Vesta was one of the most important in Roman religion. Her priestesses, the Vestals, or Vestal Virgins, therefore took an oath of chastity for their 30-year term of service tending to the ever-burning sacred fire of Rome, Vesta's sacred hearth, as well as other rites.

Vestals accused of breaking that oath were judged by the high priest of Rome. Since a priestess was a sacred person, her blood could not be shed. If found guilty, the priestess was buried alive, with a lamp and a little food, and left to the judgment of Vesta. If any condemned Vestal were innocent, it was believed that surely the goddess would free her from her living death, which began in the Middle Ages

In medieval Europe, Christians continued to take oaths. The religious and secular worlds were closely interconnected for most of these centuries, and most oaths referred to Christian beliefs.

In the early Middle Ages, Christians took oaths in the name of God, often while holding a religious object like a relic of a saint or a book of the Gospels. In most cases, oaths were not strictly person-to-person but involved the wider community in some important way. Kings took coronation oaths, swearing to rule justly and safeguard the people of the kingdom; lesser nobles took oaths of fealty to greater nobles, often for protection and material advantage.

Religious leaders like bishops and abbots also became part of this oath-based system, since there was a secular jurisdiction over important tracts of land. Breaking an oath was believed to bring down the wrath of God in time, but other than that, upholding one's personal honor and reputation within the local community was a key consideration.

Until the early 13th century, Christian rites would accompany the earlier Germanic practice of trial by ordeal. In these earlier centuries, most local people accused of a crime could be found not guilty by compurgation – that is, through oaths made by other respected members of the community testifying to the accused's honest character.

In other cases, often involving strangers to the local community, the accused could be cleared only by divine intervention. After a night of fasting and prayer, the accused would undergo a physical ordeal, like carrying a heated block of iron over a set number of steps or being thrown into a pond to sink or float.

If the accused did not develop blisters or was "accepted" by the water and sank, that was understood as God's declaration of his innocence. As time went on, scholars and ordinary people increasingly criticized the reliability of trials by ordeal. By the 13th century, the procedures of the court trial were defined and adopted, both in canon law, that is, the church law, and in secular law. Oaths matter when looking at the history of why they were developed for those serving in public office.

When drafting the U.S. Constitution in 1787, the Founding Fathers rejected some of the legal practices of the British system of law. One such rejection was of the "religious test." In Great Britain, all office holders had to affirm the religious doctrines of the Church of England. But in the independent United States, there was to be no such religious restriction placed on federal officeholders. Preserving religious liberty was a primary concern protected by the Constitution.

One of the British legal practices the Founding Fathers did include in the Constitution was the swearing of oaths upon entering federal governmental service. However, these oaths were not taken to pledge loyalty to a single monarch, but to "protect and defend" the Constitution itself, but "swearing-in ceremonies" communicate far more. Supreme Court justices take two oaths, one judicial, and the other constitutional. The oath ceremony is still a serious performative utterance.

Appointees take these oaths in front of witnesses, who are themselves, representative of the entire community, the appointees will serve. Appointees to the Supreme Court commit themselves, not to a partisan political agenda, and not to a cult of personality or to the judgment of popular opinion. They commit themselves to "protect and defend the Constitution" and "administer justice without respect to persons … faithfully and impartially."

Justices might be impeached by Congress for failing in "good behavior." However, in practice, justices serve for life, until death or retirement, and are bound in good conscience to carry out their "duties" as they have sworn to do. It is the conscience of appointees, not the preservation of their reputations, has been that the focus of these "oaths of office" for approximately 250 years.

Chapter Eleven: Loyalty Oaths

The laws receive their force and authority from an oath of
fidelity, either tacit or expressed, which living subjects have
sworn to their oversteer to restrain the intestine fermentation of
the private interest of individuals.

— Cesare Beccaria

A loyalty oath is a declaration by an individual of
allegiance to a government and its institutions and a
disavowal of support for foreign ideologies or associations.
The constitutionality of loyalty oaths is part of the larger
struggle between the power of government to regulate
perceived threats to national security and the First
Amendment rights of citizens to speak and to associate
freely. Over the history of early America, Loyalty Oaths
were essential, since they helped the United States when it
became a self-governing republic. Oaths of loyalty to the
new political system became an important tool in helping
sustain it.

In Article 2, cl. 8 of the U.S. Constitution requires
the President to take an oath of office. Article 4, cl. 3
requires oaths of office for members of the U.S. Congress;
the federal judiciary; and officers of state legislative,
executive, and judicial branches of government. Loyalty

oaths also played an important part in the naturalization process. Persons born in the United States are citizens by birth, but resident aliens who wish to become citizens must first swear an oath of allegiance to the United States.

During and after World Wars, the government enacted loyalty oaths for employees. Loyalty oaths have been regarded as essential tools in the defense of the United States from its enemies from both within and outside the country, this was especially true during wartime. Both during and after World War I and World War II, along with during the Cold War, widespread fear of communism, fascism, and socialism, and the concomitant anxiety of ensuring that Americans were and would remain loyal to the United States, led federal and state governments to enact legislation to weed out subversive organizations and those who supported them.

It was then that Congress aggressively investigated the loyalty of citizens, notably through the special House Un-American Activities Committee (HUAC) and the Senate Permanent Investigation Subcommittee. The HUAC enacted statutes, such as the Smith Act of 1940 and the 1950 McCarran Internal Security Act, which looked to increase the rise of communism in the United States. Both federal and state governments also enacted security programs that included loyalty oaths for government employees and members of labor unions and professional organizations.

Supreme Court struck down mandatory flag salute for West Virginia schoolchildren

The Pledge of Allegiance is a form of loyalty oath. State laws requiring students to salute the American flag and recite the Pledge of Allegiance in public schools led to the Supreme Court's landmark decision in West Virginia State Board of Education v. Barnette in 1943, which struck down West Virginia's mandatory flag salute statute as a violation of the First Amendment. The continued popularity of the Pledge of Allegiance as an avowal of patriotism is apparent in the ongoing conflict over its wording. However, not all loyalty oath cases are based on First Amendment.

The Supreme Court had decided many cases involving public employees' loyalty oaths, but not all were decided solely on First Amendment grounds. Some were based on due process rights, and others were based on the Fifth Amendment's privilege against self-incrimination. At one time, the Supreme Court first interpreted the constitutionality of loyalty oaths right after the Civil War, it declared them ex post facto laws and bills of attainder.

Although the Court looked at 'clear and present danger' to government interest in considering loyalty oath.

In loyalty oath cases involving the First Amendment, the government has been able to constitutionally require loyalty oaths of public employees, but the wording of the oath is all-important. The oath must specifically define and punish behavior that constitutes a clear and present danger to a substantial government interest. This includes not infringing on the First and Fourteenth Amendment right, along with an oath must not be so vague that those hearing it need to guess at its meaning. The oath must also not be a condition on employment or engage in activities where protected speech is taking place.

Chapter Twelve: Test Oaths

Holding office often requires swearing an oath to support and defend the Constitution of the United States against all enemies, foreign and domestic. Running for office should include accepting responsibility for this, too, so that our democratic republic's underpinnings can remain strong for generations to come.

— Eric Swalwell

I do solemnly swear that I will support and defend the Constitution of the United States against all enemies, foreign and domestic; that I will bear true faith and allegiance to the same; that I take this obligation freely, without any mental reservation or purpose of evasion; and that I will well and faithfully discharge the duties of the office on which I am about to enter. So help me God.

At the start of each new Congress, in January of every odd-numbered year, one-third of senators take an oath when beginning a new term into public office. While the oath-taking practice dates back to the First Congress in 1789, the current oath is a product of the 1860s, drafted during the Civil War.

The Constitution contains an oath of office for the president of the United States. For other officials, including members of Congress, that document specifies only that they "shall be bound by Oath or Affirmation to support this constitution." In 1789 the First Congress adopted a simple oath: "I do solemnly swear that I will support the Constitution of the United States."

At the outbreak of the Civil War in April of 1861, a time of uncertain and shifting loyalties, President Abraham Lincoln ordered all federal civilian employees within the executive branch to take an expanded oath. After its emergency session that summer, Congress adopted legislation requiring executive branch employees to take the expanded oath in support of the Union. In July 1862 Congress added a new section to the oath, which became known as the "Ironclad Test Oath." The Test Oath required civilian and military officials to swear or affirm that they had never aided or encouraged "persons engaged in armed hostility" against the United States. Government employees who swore falsely would be prosecuted for perjury and forever denied federal employment. Congress also revised the rest of the oath with language that closely resembles the modern oath.

It wasn't until January 1864 where the Senate adopted a resolution that required all senators to take the Test Oath. The resolution also required senators to "subscribe" to the oath by signing a printed copy. This condition reflected a wartime practice in which military and civilian authorities required anyone wishing to do business with the federal government to sign a copy of the Test Oath. The current practice of newly sworn senators signing individual pages in an elegantly bound oath book dates from this period.

After the Civil War, Congress permitted some former Confederates to take only the second section of the 1862 oath, and an 1868 statute prescribed this alternative oath for "any person who has participated in the late rebellion, and from whom all legal disabilities arising therefrom have been removed by an act of Congress.

Northerners complained of the law's unfair double standard that required loyal Unionists to take the Test Oath's harsh first section while permitting ex-Confederates to ignore it. In 1884, after more than a decade of such complaints, a new generation of lawmakers repealed the first section of the Test Oath, leaving intact today's affirmation of constitutional allegiance.

A Test Oath is when someone is inaugurated to public office, he or she takes the "oath of office. It argues that no one should be permitted to hold public office who does not take a "test oath."

There are two definitions of "test oath" to be found in American legal history. The subject can be confusing because some court cases have used both definitions indiscriminately.

- An ordinary oath is a declaration that the oath-taker believes in God and that He will judge falsehood and broken promises.
- A "Test Oath" affirms further loyalty. In the past, this additional loyalty was to a king or a church.

Today, any oath which has an explicit reference to one's religious beliefs is often called a test oath. The history behind test oaths started in the Middle Ages, kings, princes, and feudal lords demanded oaths of loyalty from their vassals. Not just to the prince, but to his religion as well. After the Reformation, if a prince became a Lutheran, everyone in his realm became a Lutheran. By law. Anyone accepting a political office or public trust took an oath of loyalty to the prince and to their faith.

In America, many of the colonies limited political offices to members of the Church of England, or other denominations. After the Revolution against Britain, very few people wanted their tax dollars to pay the salaries of the clergy for the Church of England (no surprise). But which denomination would be supported by taxes and oaths? The colonists decided to eliminate taxes and oaths which favored any particular denomination. Before the Constitution was written, every state had eliminated the requirement that public office holders be members of a particular denomination. The Revolution rather than the First Amendment effectively marked the end of test oaths and "established churches."

While every state still required that politicians believe in GOD. Non-believers could not take an oath. An oath was a declaration of belief in God. The oath taker declares that he believes in God and that he is fully aware that God will judge him if what he says is false or if what he promises is not fulfilled.

At the time the Constitution was ratified, these two points were universally understood:

- An oath could be taken only by someone who believed in God.

- An oath of office could be taken by anyone who believed in God, regardless of denominational affiliation. In short, no other "religious test" would be required.

Both before and after the Constitution was ratified, the states required candidates to be Biblically qualified to take the oath of office. They were not required to affirm their membership in a particular denomination, but they were required to swear that they were Christians. If you were not a Christian, you could not hold office.

As an example, see the Delaware Constitution, Art. 22 (adopted Sept. 20, 1776):

> Every person who shall be chosen a member of either house,
> or appointed to any office or place of trust . . .
> shall . . . make and subscribe the following declaration, to wit:
> "I _____, do profess faith in God the Father, and in Jesus Christ His only Son,
> and in the Holy Ghost, one God, Blessed for evermore;
> and I do acknowledge the Holy scripture

of the Old and New, Testaments to be
given by divine inspiration."

All states required Christian belief before the
American Revolution. There was no other "religious test."
The U.S. Constitution banned "religious tests." Article VI,
para. 3 reads:

> The Senators and Representatives before
> mentioned, and the members of the several state
> legislatures, and all executive and judicial officers,
> both of the United States and of the several states,
> shall be bound by oath or affirmation, to support
> this Constitution; but no religious test shall ever be
> required as a qualification to any office or public
> trust under the United States.

At this point in time, the requirement of "an oath" was a
requirement of an act of religious worship, a solemn
declaration made in the presence of God. The option to
"affirm" rather than "swear" was included for the benefit of
Quakers, who would not take an oath, but did believe in
God. The debates in the state ratifying conventions indicate
that many Ratifiers understood the paragraph to be
speaking of what might be called a "denominational" test.

No one would be required to be a member of a particular church/denomination. They assumed office-holders would be Christian. After drafting the Constitution, the Signers returned to their home states and drafted state constitutions that limited public office to Christians. In their minds, the Constitution did not change anything but merely protected what already existed.

Some scholars have argued that this provision applies only to Federal Offices, but not to state offices. In other words, the states would still be free to limit state offices to Episcopalians, if they so choose. However, the states had already ended this practice anyway. They didn't want the federal government to give privileges to who-knows-what denomination over the others.

On the other hand, the debates indicate some were concerned that an atheist could become President. In reply, men like Theophilus Parsons of Newburyport, MA, said Americans would *never* vote for an atheist, but an oath would be of no use because an atheist would simply lie or swear falsely that he was a Christian. The U.S. Supreme Court Justice Joseph Story, whose Commentaries on the Constitution were recognized as the most authoritative statement of the meaning of the Constitution, declared that as a result of this Article, "the Calvinist . . . and the Infidel may sit down at the common table of the national councils without any inquisition into their faith or mode of worship."

Today, Test Oaths no longer exist, since every form of oath is dead. Justice Story and other constitutional authorities have given secularists ammunition with which to attack the Christian roots of our legal system. The doctrine of church and state took generations to construct. It is not found in the text of the Constitution. This is because of this doctrine, secularists today argue that any religious content at all in an oath is "unconstitutional." Secularists call the requirement that political of office holders believe in God a "test oath." But it was not until 1961 that the U.S. Supreme Court declared a requirement to believe in God unconstitutional. This led to the decision a few months later to ban prayer and Bible reading from the states' schools.

The Constitution does not require it, virtually every President since Washington has added the words "so help me, God" to his oath of office, indicating that they did not believe Article VI required completely secular oaths. But a strange thing has happened. A very strange thing. Although secularists were able to get "test oaths" declared unconstitutional in 1961, many legislatures and courts still require the use of the phrase "so help me, God" in all oaths. Atheists have gone to court on several occasions seeking to have this phrase eliminated.

They were logical to do so; the doctrine of the "separation of church and state" as articulated by the Supreme Court demands secular oaths. But courts were reluctant to face the adverse publicity such a decision would have. What they did was declare that the phrase "so help me, God" does not refer to God! One court said it had no theological purpose. However, without directly ruling on the issue, the U.S. Supreme Court has called the phrase "ceremonial deism." Back in the days of "test oaths," that same Court denounced as a form of *unbelief*. Many, many Christians have since taken an oath which the United States Supreme Court has defined as an acknowledgment that the oath taker would is an unbeliever. Christians must take steps to release themselves from these secular oaths and take a Christian "test oath." To do so would be to repudiate the entire edifice of secular church-state theory the courts have built over the years.

According to the U.S. Supreme Court, the oath is a formality today for those serving in public office, as predicted many years prior by George Washington. It "simply" requires the candidate to take a secular "oath" that he will "support the constitution" and perform his job "to the best of my ability." As a result, most people have sworn to "support the constitution" that they may not ever read before. Life and property are now threatened by the government, whose officers no longer have Godly reputations. It becomes necessary to restore the "test oath." Not out of loyalty to political parties, but rather as an allegiance to God.

Webster's 1828 edition of the *American Dictionary of the English Language* defines "oath" as follows: A solemn affirmation or declaration, made with an appeal to God for the truth of what is affirmed. The appeal to God in an oath implies that the person imprecates His vengeance and renounces His favor if the declaration is false, or if the declaration is a promise, the person invokes the vengeance of God if he should fail to fulfill it. A false oath is called perjury.

Chapter Thirteen: Faith in Public Office

The very word 'secrecy' is repugnant in a free and open society;
and we are as a people inherently and historically opposed to
secret societies, secret oaths, and to secret proceedings.

— John F. Kennedy

Oaths of office are strangely ubiquitous in liberal-democratic regimes. They bind officeholders to their duties of office, but they do so by invoking divine or religious sanction for the performance of those duties. This divine witness to the oath of office appears to stand in as a guarantor of the political order but also looms large as an authority that is separate from, and in some sense stands above, the political order.

This opens up the possibility that this other sovereign may make moral demands that supersede those of the political order and the duties incumbent upon the office holder.

This is the paradox of the oath of office. It both guarantees the performance of official duties and subjects the content of those duties to external judgment. It is a paradox embedded in the very nature of the oath of office, which captures within its short compass the very large question of the relationship between religious conviction, moral principle, and political power.

Through a study of the use of oaths in our political systems. This includes their secular adaptation, the affirmation of office, much light can be shed on the nature of faith in public office and its Oaths.

Oaths of office come to us as vestiges of a previous age, or so it seems. They belong to a time when duty was before right and religious sanction was taken for granted. During an era when the whole of morality turned on the discharge of one's moral duties, and the very foundation of justice was truth and fidelity to promises and agreements. Many countries such as Australia, treat oaths differently than the United States.

During an age when witnessed oaths cemented office-holders to the burdens of responsibility. Although despite this seeming distance from our own time, oaths and affirmations remain a ubiquitous presence in our public law and government administration. At her coronation ceremony the Queen promised under oath to govern the peoples of the United Kingdom and her overseas possessions according to their respective laws and customs; to cause law and justice, in mercy, to be executed in all her judgments; and to maintain the laws of God and the true profession of the gospel within the United Kingdom. The Governor-General promised under oath that he would be faithful and bear true allegiance to Her Majesty Queen Elizabeth the Second," and well and truly serve her Majesty … in the office of Governor-General, and would do right to all manner of people after the laws and usages of the Commonwealth of Australia, without fear or favor, affection or ill will. All elected members of the Australian Parliament are required to swear or solemnly affirm their allegiance to the Queen, and the Prime Minister, Ministers, and Parliamentary Secretaries take an oath or affirmation of office and the executive counselor's oath or affirmation.

Justices of the High Court of Australia, like the judges of all Australian courts, are required to affirm or swear a similar oath of allegiance and service to the Queen and to promise to do right to all manner of people according to law without fear or favor, affection or ill-will. Witnesses in Australian courts are required to give evidence under oath or affirmation that the evidence they will give will be the truth, the whole truth, and nothing but the truth, and jurors are required to swear or affirm that they will give a true verdict according to the evidence.

Contemporary Australian law allows for affirmations instead of oaths, and statutory declarations instead of sworn affidavits in most circumstances, and oaths can now be taken in a manner consistent with the oath-taker's religion. Although these developments suggest a kind of "secularization" of Australian law and politics, it seems that the policy issues that arise today are more about accommodating religious diversity than they are about removing religion from public life.

The exact terms of the minister's oath of office have been changed five times in recent years: under Prime Ministers Paul Keating, John Howard, Kevin Rudd, Julia Gillard, and Tony Abbott; and the executive councilor's oath or affirmation was also changed under Prime Ministers Malcolm Fraser and Paul Keating. The main points of difference between these oaths and affirmations concerned whether the relevant promises were made to "the Queen," to "the Commonwealth of Australia," or to "the people of Australia."

If Australia had become a republic following the referendum in 1999, a new oath or affirmation would have been expected of the President and members of Parliament, requiring them to swear loyalty to the Commonwealth and the people.

The language of oaths is sometimes quite unusual to modern ears. In colonial New South Wales, each Justice of the Peace swore to "do equal right to the poor and the rich after my cunning, wit, and power, and after the laws and customs of the realm and statutes made thereof." This reflected the language of an oath required by Henry VIII in the thirty-fifth year of his reign, which called upon the swearer to promise with all of his "Body, Cunning, Wit, and uttermost ... Power," and "without Guile, Fraud, or other undue Mean," that he would "observe, keep, maintain, and defend all of the King's Majesty's Stiles, Titles and Rights" with "the whole Effects and Contents of the Acts provided for the same, and all other Acts and Statutes made, or to be made, with this Realm," together with "the Derogation, Extirpation, and Extinguishment of the usurped and pretended Authority, Power, and Jurisdiction of the See and Bishop of Rome, and all other Foreign Potentates."

Although they seem archaic throwbacks to a bygone era, oaths of office clearly matter. A person is not able to enter into public office and exercise official power until an appropriate oath or affirmation is duly made.

Chapter Fourteen: Acts of Religion

When I place my hand on the Bible and take the oath of office,
that oath becomes my highest promise to God.

— Mitt Romney

An oath is an act of religion. Thomas Aquinas said that oaths were an act of latria or worship, the special reverence that is due to God alone. John Calvin called oaths a "species of divine worship," an act of "religious veneration." The Torah had thundered: "Thou shalt fear the LORD thy God, and serve him, and shalt swear by his name" (Deuteronomy 6:13). For, as the Letter to the Hebrews put it, "men swear 'y one greater than themselves, and with them, an oath given as confirmation is an end of every dispute" (6:16). The Qur'an warns: "those who exchange the covenant of Allah and their oaths for a small price will have no share in the Hereafter, and Allah will not speak to them or look at them on the Day of Resurrection, nor will He purify them, and they will have a painful punishment" (Sura 3:77). Although Jesus Christ countered all this when he said: "do not swear at all ... but let your 'Yes' be 'Yes', and your 'No', 'No'" (Matthew 5:33-37). Relying on this saying, the Quakers refused to take oaths at all, and there is a wonderful statement by Voltaire to the effect that the compact entered into by William Penn with his American neighbors was the only such treaty "that was not ratified by an oath, and was never infringed. Even the refusal of an oath was for the Quakers an act of religion.

Thomas Hobbes argued that an oath adds nothing to obligations that already exist: a covenant, if lawful, binds the conscience with or without an oath; whereas an unlawful covenant is not binding even if confirmed by oath. Moses Mendelssohn, the great German philosopher of the Jewish Enlightenment, agreed that an oath adds nothing to the obligations that already exist, namely, the duty to tell the truth and to keep one's promises. The taking of an oath, he maintained, serves neither for a conscientious man nor for a determined profligate. The former already knows that God is a witness to everything he says and does; the latter has no conscience and will readily swear a false oath and lie. All that the oath does, he said, is to fortify the irresolute and wavering to those who have principles, but do not always live up to them.

Immanuel Kant said something similar. The oath, he argued, presumes that a man who is not disposed to tell the truth will nonetheless be persuaded to do so by calling divine punishment down upon himself, "just as though it rested upon him whether or not to render account to this supreme tribunal." The oath is a kind of "spiritual torture," Kant said, which might be justified pragmatically, but that is all. It would be better if we told the truth because it is simply the right thing to do. For such a people, no oath is needed.

Certainly, the abuse of oaths can be very great. Under the Weimar Constitution of 1919, members of the German military swore loyalty to the Reich Constitution and pledged obedience to it. After Adolf Hitler was appointed Chancellor in 1933, however, the oath of loyalty was reframed so that it was addressed to the People and the Fatherland, and when the offices of Chancellor and President were merged in 1934, it was further transformed into an oath of personal loyalty to Adolf Hitler himself – as Leader of the German Empire and People.

This personal oath of loyalty to the Fuhrer was required of civil servants and government officials, including university professors and church pastors. Karl Barth, the famous Professor of Theology, then at the University of Bonn, refused to take the oath unless it was clearly understood to be subject to his prior responsibilities to God as an Evangelical Christian. Without this qualification, he argued, a promise of unlimited obedience would treat Hitler as if he were some kind of "a god incarnate.

Under the extreme pressure of the time, however, the Confessing Church stated that because an oath involves an acknowledgment of God as a divine witness, it necessarily excludes "any actions which would be contrary to God's command attested in Holy Scripture." On this understanding, Barth decided he could take the oath, but he was nevertheless dismissed from his post at the University for raising the issue in the first place and was soon forced to leave the country. From his native Switzerland, he continued to question the loyalty oath as purporting to displace the unqualified loyalty owed by a Christian to the Lord Jesus Christ.

Dietrich Bonhoeffer, who was later killed for his courageous opposition to Nazism and his role in the attempt to assassinate Hitler, was not required to take the oath because he was already deemed an illegal pastor, but he attempted to convince his fellow pastors not to do so. For Bonhoeffer, "no earthly obligation is absolutely binding" and it was therefore illegitimate to take any oath which made an "unconditional demand" after the style of the Hitler oath.

Adolf Eichmann, an infamous SS Officer found guilty of crimes against humanity, war crimes, and crimes against the Jewish people for his role in the organization of the Holocaust, had no such scruples. At his trial, he infamously excused his behavior as the carrying out of orders. "I am guilty of having been obedient," he said, of "having subordinated myself to my official duties and the obligations of war service and my oath of allegiance and my oath of office." Hannah Arendt controversially perceived a "banality of evil" in Eichmann's wooden and obtuse responses to questioning, but Bettina Stangneth has recently argued that Eichmann was far from a mindless functionary, hardly have "a small cogged in Adolf Hitler's extermination machine" as he had maintained throughout his office.

Chapter Fifteen: Dark Oaths

Unfortunately, in today's world, we have to be reminded that the power of an oath derives from the fact that in it we ask God to bear witness to the promises we make with the implicit expectation that He will hold us accountable for the manner in which we honor them.

— James L. Buckley

Dark oaths can also be conspiratorial and subversive. Tacitus records the promises extracted from the Batavian chiefs by the one-eyed Gaius Julius Civilis, who collected them "at a sacred grove under the pretext of giving a banquet," persuaded them to join his revolt, and then "bound them all by their national forms of oath and barbarous rites." Rembrandt depicts the scene memorably in his dark, grotesque, and mordant Conspiracy of Claudius Civilis (1661-62). Members of the city council of Amsterdam, who had commissioned the painting to celebrate the construction of their new town hall, seem not to have been amused.

Life and death. Judgment of the body in this life and the soul in the hereafter. It is difficult to overestimate the significance of the oath. Was Jacques Derrida exaggerating when he said that the oath makes a promise that human language cannot undo? In the Merchant of Venice, Shylock regarded himself as bound by his oath to perform his promise to extract a proverbial pound of flesh from Antonio upon default of that infamous loan. Commenting on the binding power of the oath, Derrida wrote:

"The oath, the sworn faith, the act of swearing is transcendence itself, the experience of passing beyond man, the origin of the divine or if one prefers, the divine origin of the oath."

Carl Schmitt is famous for the claim that all of the important ideas in our modern liberal politics are secularized theological concepts. Schmidt had the idea of sovereignty, especially in mind, but he might just as easily have been talking about the oath and the solemn affirmation. Derrida suggested just this when he observed that even when God is not named, that is, even in the most secular pledge of commitment, His Presence is nonetheless implicitly invoked.

Charles Barbour, following Derrida, locates within our language and communication a whole array of theological concepts that haunt our ostensibly secular modernity. All social, political, and legal relations, he argues, are structured by something like an oath, a mutual promise to trust each other's word. The problem that the oath addresses concerns what he calls "the opacity of the other" – the mundane fact that we cannot know what another is thinking and must therefore accept their promises on trust. Our reliance on oaths and solemn affirmations is testimony to the faith that we must invest in each other, especially those who rule over us. It was not necessary to venture too deeply into the labyrinth of post-modern philosophy to see the point. An implied promise of fidelity is presupposed by human communication. Oaths of office propose to externalize and formalize this act of faith. In so doing, they purport to domesticate what has been called that wild or vast notion of what in every man's conception is just or unjust.

Chapter Sixteen: Locations of Sovereignty

As lawmakers, we swore an oath to protect and defend the Constitution.

— Conor Lamb

Oaths and affirmations of office track the ebb and flow of ultimate authority and binding power within societies and cultures. They simultaneously reveal the location of our highest religious commitments and the grounds upon which the coercive powers of government are exercised.

The ancient civilizations of the Mediterranean basin Babylon, Egypt, Assyria, Greece, Rome, and many others were related to each other through treaty covenants sworn before their respective gods.

Many of these treaty covenants, were not agreements among equals but were rather the terms of a hegemonic relationship between suzerain and vassal. As scholars such as Peter Karavites and Moshe Weinfeld have shown, although the specific terms and rituals differed from one culture to another, the structural similarities point to a common origin and a shared set of understandings about the role of oaths in binding kings and nations to their obligations. Under conditions of polytheism, the gods of all the relevant nations were invoked as witnesses to the treaties.

The practice of confirming international treaties with an oath continued after the Christianization of the Roman Empire but was based on a shared monotheism. It was not until some point after the Enlightenment that this practice came to an end. As Allen Hertz has pointed out, thereafter the binding force of international treaties had to depend upon a natural law obligation to keep one's promises, or else the geo-political self-interest of states and the threat of military intervention.

The Germanic peoples of Europe placed a great deal of emphasis on the oath. A person charged with wrongdoing could rebut the charge by swearing an oath of innocence. It might also be determined that a person charged with a debt must prove his innocence with the assistance of twelve or more oath-helpers who would swear to their belief in the defendant's oath.

The reasons for the decline in this practice, which was called canonical purgation in ecclesiastical courts and wager of law in the common law courts – are complicated and obscure. It made some sense in local communities where personal reputation as a real constraint on behavior, as well as a means by which the secret sexual sins of clergy and accusations of adultery might be addressed within ecclesiastical law, but these considerations did not apply to the common law administered by the royal courts at Westminster. Over time, compurgation was displaced by trial by jury and the testimonial oath, which had been institutionalized in Roman jurisprudence as early as Emperor Constantine, who erroneously believed he was following Christian practice by requiring witness statements to be sworn on oath.

Oaths were certainly a mainstay of medieval civilization. One only has to list them: oaths of homage and allegiance, oaths of chivalry, oaths of fraternity, vows of pilgrimage, chastity or celibacy, oaths of jurors and office-holders. The emergent towns and cities of medieval Europe, Harold Berman observes, were "religious associations in the sense that each was held together by religious values and rituals, including religious oaths." The charters by which the cities were established were "confirmed by religious oaths, and the oaths, which were renewed with successive installations of officers, included, above all, vows to uphold the municipal laws."

The oath-bound confederation was a common institution of medieval Europe where the rise of social contract theory – the idea that state authority is based on an agreement among the people – cannot be understood apart from this context. However, it was oaths of a rather different kind – oaths of fealty, allegiance, and abjuration – which came into their own as tools of European statecraft during the tumultuous sixteenth and seventeenth centuries.

To imagine a ruler succeeding to the throne based on a solemn oath was very consistent with the Reformation insistence on the importance of secular vocations, through which every layman was called directly into the service of God. But in the hands of Henry VIII, the oath of allegiance functioned as a potent means of maintaining control over his subjects. As Thea Cervone pointed out: rather than describing fealty to the monarch, Henry VIII wished for the Oaths of Supremacy and Succession to describe fealty to him." Another observed: "The Tudor state had succeeded to the church's role as arbiter of the individual conscience and then set about investing loyalty oaths with obligations arising from conscience.

A multitude of oaths and subscriptions were used by Henry VIII to secure his new divorce, the succession of the throne, and his supremacy over the English church. One only has to mention the oaths associated with Henry VIII's Act of Succession in 1534 and Elizabeth I's later Act of

Supremacy, and James I's Popish Recusants Act to recognize the significance of the oath in Tudor and Stuart statecraft.

Elizabeth I had a supremacy oath was required of every archbishop, bishop, and all and every other ecclesiastical person and "every temporal judge, justice, mayor, and other lay or temporal officer and minister. Under the oath, the promisor was required to declare that the queen was "the only supreme governor" over the realm and all her majesty's overseas dominions, not only in temporal affairs, but also in all spiritual or ecclesiastical matters. The oath-taker was also required to swear that "no foreign prince, person, prelate, state or potentate has, or ought to have" any jurisdiction within the realm, and had to "utterly renounce and forsake all foreign jurisdictions, powers, superiorities, and authorities."

James, I had an oath of allegiance that further required the swearer to deny the power of the pope to depose the king or authorize armed rebellion against him, and to deny any such effect to any sentence of ex-communication of the king. Sir Thomas More and Bishop John Fisher were executed precisely because they refused to take Henry VIII's oath of succession, particularly as it required the oath-taker to abjure "any foreign potentate," which was to impugn the authority of the pope in favor of the king.

The oath, says one scholar, thus became an irresistibly attractive tool of the authorities. For it is a powerful, infrangible, obligation that can bind the individual to the big political entities, the nation, and the national church.

William Shakespeare well recognized this, as the pivotal role of oaths, vows, and conscriptions in his many plays attests. Now oaths are so frequent, since the mid-seventeenth century, they should be taken like pills, swallowed whole: if you chew them you will find them bitter: if you think of what you swear, twill hardly go down. The ex officio oath which required defendants to swear to answer questions even if their answers might incriminate them was a particularly useful tool in the hands of the Star Chamber and High Commission.

It was a procedure whereby a charge of heresy could be pursued even where there were no independent witnesses when the defendant was accused instead by clamosa insinuatio that is by 'public scandal'. In such a case the judge or ordinary was empowered to act ex officio and to ask the accused to take an oath to answer truthfully and absolutely any question that was asked of him. There was no specific bill of charges, no indictment providing the limits of allowable questioning. There was also no legal counsel for the accused. The judge effectively took the part also of prosecution and even of defense. The odds against the accused in such circumstances were catastrophic. Unless he was himself an expert in theology, he was virtually certain to convict himself of some heresy or other under such open rules of examination.

William Tyndale, like many Protestant reformers who followed him, objected to the use of state power to inquire into the private beliefs and thoughts in this way. He argued that judgment ought to proceed only based on evidence sworn by witnesses, and should not presume to inquire into men's consciences:

> "in the causes that are brought to them, when they sit in God's stead, let them judge and condemn the trespasser under lawful witnesses … Let what is known only to God, and of which no proof can be made or lawful witness brought, abide until the coming of the Lord, who will reveal all secrets … God has given them no further authority."

The Star Chamber and High Commission were abolished by the Habeas Corpus Act and High Commission Abolition Act, and the erection of such courts was denounced by the

Bill of Rights as being illegal and pernicious. The privilege against self-incrimination enjoyed by defendants today is largely a result of the common law's reaction against the use of the ex officio oath.

Oaths of office and oaths of allegiance have been the example of state authority. They have determined its metes and bounds, and continue to do so. During the English civil war, publicists of all perspectives found it necessary to address the question of the oath as a way of identifying the proper bounds of the authority of the king, the parliament, and the people.

James I had maintained that only God could enforce the coronation oath against the king, and Philip Hunton argued that the people continue to owe obedience to the king under their oaths of subjection. On the other hand, Samuel Rutherford insisted that if the "oath betwixt the king and his people" is broken, "the party injured is loosed from the contract" and the people operating through their inferior magistrates may resist tyranny on the part of the king.

Anthony Ascham, like Thomas Hobbes, later argued that self-preservation is the most basic obligation so that no oath could oblige the oath taker to comply with his oath if that should prejudice his own safety and that the oath binds him no more than he intended to be bound when taking the oath. However, Robert Sanderson, who was chaplain to Charles I, responded that this would tend, among other things:

> "To the bringing in of atheism, with the contempt of God and all religion, whilst every man, by making his preservation the measure of all his duties and actions, makes himself thereby his own idol."

The sentence of Oliver Cromwell's High Court of Justice, which convicted Charles I of high treason, was premised specifically on the "trust, oath, and office" committed to him – to be used, it was said, for the "good of the people" and for the "preservation of their liberties," and not to erect in himself an "unlimited and tyrannical power to rule according to his will." While those involved in the trial and execution of the king were later themselves executed for regicide and the breach of their own duties of loyalty, the assertion of the Parliament's ultimate control over the terms of the coronation oath, the succession to the Crown and the oath of allegiance were crucial to the establishment of its sovereignty as a result of the "glorious revolution" of 1688-1689. Thus were established the constitutional assumptions of Australian law and government.

Chapter Seventeen: Allegiance and Sovereignty

On my first day in Washington, I swore an oath of office to the Constitution of the United States, and it is and always will be the foundation for every vote I take.

— Nancy Mace

In more recent times, in Australia, differing views about the nature and location of sovereignty have been at the heart of changes to the oaths of office and oaths of allegiance required of our public officials. However, sovereignty is a notoriously ambiguous and contested concept. For a start: is it vested in the Queen, the Parliament, or the Australian people? The constitutional answer to this question is far from clear, and the terms of the oaths and affirmations of office within the various Australian jurisdictions reflect this ambiguity. And what is the role and status of our judges in this context? One may have to ask whether today's judges, exercising vast powers of judicial review over legislation and executive action, are always faithful to their oath-bound obligation to do justice "according to law."

Sir Gerard Brennan had occasion on his swearing-in as Chief Justice of the High Court of Australia to reflect on the judicial oath as the ground upon which he was obliged to do justice according to law and not according to his own view of what the law ought to be, which was "that wild or vast notion of what in every man's conception is just or unjust."

Paolo Prodi has argued that "the early modern state's monopolization of oaths represents a socialization of power in the first step towards a 'secular oath'." In this connection, it may be worth recalling Dietrich Bonhoeffer's observation that there are two ways in which untruthfulness can undermine an oath: "either it may actually insinuate itself into the oath, or else disguise itself in the form of an oath by invoking some secular or divine power instead of the living God."

The religious oath may be a ready tool in the hands of the political authorities from Henry VIII to Adolf Hitler – but its complete secularization can also mark a shift toward totalitarianism. The Soviet Union had an oath, but it was an oath that invoked not God, but rather the "stern punishment of Soviet law" and the "universal hatred and contempt" of the proletariat. Joseph Stalin promulgated the following oath of allegiance for members of the Red Army:

> "I, a citizen of the Union of Soviet Socialist
> Republics, joining the ranks of the Workers' and
> Peasants' Red Army, do hereby take the oath of
> allegiance and do solemnly vow to be an honest,

brave, disciplined and vigilant fighter, to guard strictly all military and State secrets, to obey implicitly all Army regulations and orders of my commanders, commissars, and superiors … And if through evil intent I break this solemn oath, then let the stern punishment of the Soviet law, and the universal hatred and contempt of the working people, fall upon me."

Aleksandra Solzhenitsyn testified to what the stern punishment of Soviet law looked like in practice. In his accounts of Soviet justice, there is very little reference to the sworn testimony of witnesses, and much more about endless interrogations, exquisite tortures, and forced confessions.

An oath may be a kind of spiritual torture, as Kant said, but it respects the internal domain of a person's conscience as something known and judged by God alone. In a review of Giorgio Agamben's The Sacrament of Language: An Archaeology of the Oath, Justin Clemens observes:

"It is thus no wonder today, when the oath has fallen into desuetude that torture is explicitly back on the agenda even for those democratic states which had prided themselves on their thoroughgoing rejection of it. Without any trust in oaths – indeed, having repudiated almost altogether their function and efficacy – our contemporary materialist polities can imagine no other recourse than direct psycho-physical incursions into bodies in a forlorn and terrifying attempt to extract 'reliable' 'information'."

If this is so, the advice given to early Anglo-Saxon kings by Dunstan, Archbishop of Canterbury believed that may have been worth recalling, as he said:

> "The justice of a consecrated king is that he condemns no man [unjustly]; and that he defend and protect widows and orphans and foreigners; …have the old and wise and temperate as his counsellors, and appoint righteous men as officers; because, whatever they do unjustly by means of his might, he must give a reckoning on judgment day for all of it."

The Code of Emperor Justinian spoke in a similar register when requiring that judges must not "permit the hearing of a process to begin unless there is a copy of the Holy

Scriptures placed before the judicial bench." It was observed that:

> "Attending in this way to the holy Scriptures and consecrated by the presence of God, they will have greater assistance in their decisions from the knowledge that they are as much judged as judging, and that judgment is more terrible for them than for the parties, since the weighing of a litigant's cause is a matter for man's supervision, the weighing of a judge's cause is reserved for God's." In good conscience, politicians cannot overlook the Oath.

Overlooking the oath, or not recognizing it as problematic, above all because it was a religious act, has been a remarkably economical way of creating a premature secularization of political debate in which issues of office then need to be pared down to suitably secular politics, of promises and agreements and contractual rights, to conform to expectations.

There has, undoubtedly, been a Richard S. Willen, 'Rationalization of Anglo-Legal Culture: The Testimonial Oath.' The British Journal of Sociology" Secularization in our practice of oaths and affirmations. But we have to be careful about what we mean by secularization. The solemn affirmation as a substitute for the oath was originally invented for religious reasons to avoid injury to the religious consciences of Anabaptists, Quakers, and Moravians.

Even today, a clear majority of our officeholders still opt for the religious oath. Since the late 1970s, a fairly consistent figure of around 70% of senators and 75% of members of the House of Representatives have chosen to take oaths rather than solemn affirmations. And even in the most secular of states the Soviet Union a secular oath was still found to be indispensable. The chilling thing is that as fearful as the judgment of God might be, the horrors that Solzhenitsyn recounted in his Gulag Archipelago were enough of hell upon the earth as it is.

The oath of office places a limit on public power. It binds our governors to the responsibilities of the office and reminds them that they are as much judged as judging. The oath suggests that if we are to have faith in public office, we will also need to keep faith in public office.

Part III

Chapter Eighteen: Ethical Standards

The more moral the people are in their business dealings, the less
paperwork they need, the more handshakes you can have, and
the more the wheels of capitalism work better because there's
trust in the marketplace. Business ethics is not a joke. And I
think most businesses that I've dealt with encourage exactly that
type of behavior.

— Rick Santorum

Setting the bar that holds politics are its representatives to
hold themselves to ethics is an important first step to being
effective in government. Having to separate politics from
the government has not been an easy task for many in
public office. Holding to a reputation that there are no
strings attached to making decisions for their communities,
there is no room to carry themselves without a strong sense
of ethics.

Stressing the importance of open government and
keeping information available to the public are ways that
political reformers have kept a high standard of ethics.
Having little reporting efforts by the media has contributed
to too many local governments becoming corrupt. The
advancement of technology allows for greater transparency

and accountability to become a realistic goal for politicians. With the development of the World Wide Web, which began in Geneva in March 1989, when a written proposal for an Internet framework would allow online documents to link to one another. Often parallel, the World Wide Web and the movement towards accountability and transparency have become increasing in interest.

Transparency is a medium in which the way that we view things and how others view us. The belief is that more transparency increases accountability; along with published information. However, a new directive requiring stricter documentation of government meetings led to an increase in "informal lunches" where public officials can discuss topics without making their discussions publicly accessible. Such behavior could lead many to believe that public officials are discussing secrets they wish to hide from the public. Other types of technology such as social media allows for information to be shared between politicians and the people. Social media is no longer a new medium. Instead, it has become the norm for communication.

Providing solutions to encourage the people to become involved in government, the idea behind transparency is to improve engagement. It is a matter of understanding the needs of the people first before building policies.

For political reformers, holding events such as mandatory ethics training for all departments and senior staff is important to maintain trust in the government. Pieces of training such as "The Quest for Government Integrity" seminar are provided with the intention that as public officials, they share the sacred trust of public service. Administrations should be expected to fulfill such training before becoming government employees or appointed officials. This is one way to uphold trust, with the thinking that presenting such a seminar would be another way to educate city employees on the laws of local government, with Open, honest, and transparent government. This is what was pledged during his campaign. One way to achieve it was by providing ethics training as an important step in ensuring that city employees were educated and on notice about the penalties for violating ethics laws.

These were just some of the principles that are faced in political reform and governing. It's the ability to move a community forward. Over the past ten years, we are seeing a greater need for reforms to be developed. Congress has failed in recent years to enact a reform making children safer from gun violence. However, many in politics have put into place a bid specification to purchase new weaponry, with police departments becoming the majority of buyers of guns and ammunition. It was the first policy to bring about a needed expectation of what gun manufacturers owed the people when it came to their safety. As part of the policy, the government is beginning to ask all bidders the following six socially responsible questions:

- What do you do to combat illegal gun trafficking and illegal gun crime?
- Do you manufacture and sell assault weapons for civilian use?
- Do you agree not to sell certain models of firearms for civilian use?
- Are you requiring your dealers to conduct background checks?
- Do you fund research related to gun violence and smart gun technology?
- Will you commit to prohibiting your brand name from being used in violent video games?

With much skepticism, especially among gun manufacturers, ethics plays a role in decision-making. Political reformers will look for opportunities to play it forward for the people in their communities. By taking a stand on issues such as gun reform, many realize that their communities could become a little safer. The hope was that more cities and state governments would soon follow and stand boldly for the people. This is the overall thinking of a reformer. The solemn vow of politics and governing.

Chapter Nineteen: A Bright Future

The best thing about the future is that it comes one day at a time.

— Abraham Lincoln

In 2017, a new race would emerge for both Democrats and Republicans alike. With a governor that has already exhausted his terms, it will be crucial to find a candidate with fresh ideas and the ability to improve the welfare of the people. In states such as New Jersey, which has had their credit rating drop by Moody eight times in the last six years, political reform is a concern when looking at politics and government. With some longtime politicians being projected to run for public office over the next few years, it becomes imminent to find political reformers. With many key Democrats and Republicans putting their hope in their candidates to run and win, one fact remains, many have tried a run for public office and have failed.

The focus and attention on the people are to ultimately be at the forefront of any candidate's plans. Some examples of past political campaigns, such as Bret Schundler, who lost a 2001 gubernatorial bid to James McGreevey, and failed to win the GOP nomination in the 2005 governor's race. Thomas F. X. Smith stepped down as mayor in 1981 to seek the Democratic nomination for governor, losing to Jim Florio, who then lost the general election in a squeaker to Tom Kean. It was Smith's predecessor, Paul T. Jordan, who challenged then-Gov. Brendan Byrne in 1977 for the Democratic gubernatorial nomination. Byrne swamped him at the polls, and then also won the general election. In 1916, Otto Wittpenn lost his race for governor to Republican Walter Edge. Aligning with some of the best political consultants and holding to a succession of fundraising money has been shown to not be enough for political candidates. The reason may be seen as obvious, reputation.

Political experts say it's difficult for a mayor of any big city to gain supporters outside of their political base. An extra impediment for political candidates is their long-standing reputation for being a hotbed of political corruption. Many have been viewed by the people and the media for their political careers end, was seen as being sort of grubby and corrupt. However, that image has been changing, as we have seen by the past political leadership of Newark New Jersey's Cory Booker.

Throughout the projections as to the next election, political reformers continue to be engaged in trash pickup, recycling, policing, the fire department structure, healthy

147 |

living, in revamping the 911 system; along with the many challenges that the people and their communities face. There are factors to consider about the projections that a political reformer could take a chance and run in an election and win. For instance, a resume of military service, work experience in finance, prior years working in government or corporate America, and the belief that the American Dream can still exist.

With national security being a concern, along with both a crime rate and poverty levels increasing, there may be challenges to being elected, even as a reformer. In speaking with voters throughout New Jersey, another factor comes up, religion. Although political reformers can make a positive impact, there is still an unforgiving nature when it comes to voting. This is unfortunately true when looking at religion and culture. For the local government it works, unfortunately, at a state or national level, the idea falls short. It by no means is a true indication of his abilities to hold the position. It has taken approximately two hundred years for America to elect itself its first black president. As of October 2014, there have been a total of twenty-one governors in America that have been Jewish, with one currently serving, Democrat Jack Markell in Delaware. In the history of Jewish governors throughout the United

States, the people have elected twenty-four of them to date. Although this can change, other factors that many concerns that the people develop into the next grassroots campaign. The truth is, our government system has been filled by the "old school political machine," a machine that many desire to no longer exist, as the people have spent years trying to defeat it.

The positive effects of political reformers and their journeys haven't been lasting ones only for them, but instead, it has promoted an image of what a politician can have to allow them to succeed over decades.

A candidate that can bring promise, hope, and positive change to a people. In the words of the Marine motto, a reformer will leave no man or woman behind. This is how we break away from the political machine that has too often tainted politics, and develop into creating a solemn vow of political reform.

Chapter Twenty: Looking Ahead

One can lead a nation only by helping it see a bright outlook. A leader is a dealer in hope.

– Napoléon Bonaparte

In 2013, Steven has made a positive impact on the health of Jersey City. He has brought vitality, which has led the city to become one of the most progressive in the State of New Jersey. Under his leadership, Jersey City has consistently distinguished itself as being a community with inspiring accomplishments, from arts and culture to Infrastructure. Steven has brought about the change that the city needed in its years.

With more than 300 new police officers, and nearly 1500 units of affordable housing built or approved, recreation was expanded to include nearly 30 new programs and a 10 million dollar investment in parks and open space, including 800 small businesses opening, and the creation of 10,000 new jobs. Throughout his years in office, he has shown himself to be a smart, progressive leader, as he continues to open new chapters for the city. By ensuring paid sick leave, the sixth city in the United States and the first in New Jersey, Steven is ensuring that no one is left behind, a way of living for those serving in the

United States Marines. A branch of the military that Steven served in shortly after the World Trade Center bombing, by helping prisoners reenter society, and passing legislation to protect small businesses while encouraging shopping; Steven has made Jersey City a destination for all to live and work, along with being the greenest city in the nation. He has implemented a model for all law enforcement agencies for its model for diversity. Steven has led Jersey City to benefit from economic development that has benefited families at every economic level, all without raising taxes.

Over the past 12 years, Jersey City has made an unprecedented investment in building and establishing a City for everyone. Areas such as arts and culture have changed tremendously by making the City a destination not only for residents but visitors alike. In 2021, Steven announced a formal agreement with NJ Devils Entertainment to renovate the 3,000-seat Historic Loews Theater and Steven is on track for a 30 million-dollar renovation of a cultural center in the Pathside building at Journal Square. As part of the renovation, he moved to establish anchor institutions that would act as a catalyst for an expansion of the broader arts community in Jersey City, which includes working to leverage development tools that would incentivize the private sector to build permanent homes for prominent arts and cultural non-profits in Jersey City. In the fall of 2020 and into late 2021, the Nimbus Arts Center and ArtHouse Productions opened in Jersey City as welcome visitors. These were the first of several more planned theaters due to open within the next 5 years. He worked closely with the Jersey City Arts Council to enact the state's first Arts Trust Fund so that the arts community in Jersey City would for the first time have a reliable support system to expand programming while creating the most expansive and diverse mural programs in the nation, The Jersey City Mural Arts Program features 153 murals by local, regional and international artists. This includes national holidays such as the 4th of July celebration. The city established its 4th of July Festival, making the celebration one of the biggest and most exciting than ever before. Jersey City welcomes 150,000+ visitors annually to its massive Fourth of July festival of a carnival, food trucks, craft beer tastings, and the largest fireworks display in the State of New Jersey.

After two decades of restoration, the historic Van Wagenen House, otherwise known as the Apple Tree House, opened its doors to the public in 2017 and paved the way for the Jersey City Mural Arts Summer Youth Program to offer artistically inclined Jersey City youth an opportunity to apply their skills towards the creation of public art. Professional mural artists provide step-by-step instructions to young Jersey City artists on concept development, design enlargement, coherence, and spray paint techniques. To cultivate and nurture a greater appreciation for poetry and literature across the city. In November of 2018, the position of Poet Laureate was established, so to serve as Jersey City's literary arts ambassador, which grew in just two years, a collaboration with more than forty community organizations. It was the largest art and studio tour in the State of New Jersey.

Through the Jersey City Art & Studio Tour, artists have reported a 72% increase in foot traffic over the last four years due in large part to 20 new bus, bike, and walking tour experiences offered for free to the public. This led to identifying an essential tool for Jersey City by responding to the needs of the arts community, this is when Steven launched the first Cultural Asset Map in partnership with New Jersey City University and the Jersey City Arts Council in Jersey City. Currently, 413 artists and 86 organizations are registered on the map. Jersey City hosts an average of 31 flag raisings at City Hall each year, with a 35% increase in these cultural celebrations over the last 3 years.

The diversity of Jersey City has long been an important part of its landscape. Since Jersey City has long spoken about the importance of the LGBTQ community but Steven's track record is more than just talk, instead tangible and meaningful reforms have helped to strengthen the community with real resources. In 2017, the Advocate, which is recognized as the leading national LGBT publication called Jersey City the #1 queerest city in America beating out much more well-known cities like NYC and San Francisco.

In 2006, when Steven was first elected to the city council and long before marriage equality was legal in NJ Steven was a vocal and public advocate for gay marriage when few public officials were willing to endorse it. By being a believer in how government should work for the people, Steven has been an agent for change and under his leadership, Jersey City was the 1st city in New Jersey and one of the first in the country to expand its healthcare coverage to include transgender coverage. Since being elected mayor, the city has established itself as a leader on LGBTQ issues as it is one of only 3 municipalities in NJ that has received a perfect score from the Human Rights Campaign on LGBTQ issues. Jersey City is the only city in NJ to receive a perfect score for 6 consecutive years. It was one of the first cities in the country to lead with gender-neutral bathrooms essentially recognizing the importance of allowing people to use restrooms that correspond to their gender identity.

By 2016, Steven worked closely with leadership in the Jersey City Police Department to incorporate LGBT sensitivity training as part of training for all new Jersey City police officers. At the time, Jersey City was amongst the only cities in NJ to take a specific targeted approach here as part of police officer development. Since Steven took office in 2013, the team has deliberately tried to expand efforts to partner with LGBT non-profits like the Pride Center with increased resources and also providing opportunities for LGBTQ-owned businesses to partner with the city of Jersey City in creating projects that made sense for small business owners and the people living within the city.

When this project was first created, which was before Steven came into office, it was Jersey City owned a small ownership interest while Honeywell Corporation owned the majority of the Bayfront property. The plan then was only 10% of the units being affordable housing for workforce housing, but it still was a positive story as it was a major superfund site cleanup. Areas such as Jackson

Square were struggling to be revitalized. Known as "The Hub" in its Ward F, the area couldn't retain a commercial tenant, had vacancies, and was an anchor on the revitalization of the area. As mayor, Steven realized early that the past practices of the city officers renting space on the waterfront made little sense from a geography standpoint or a financial point. Over the last 3 years, he built a municipal complex in Ward F that aggregates all of our offices in one easily accessible location, moved thousands of employees to this part of the city to work, and have attracted thousands of daily city customers to the area. The results have been staggering with new businesses opening in the area, new construction for the first time in decades, and new leases being signed for small businesses, but other areas would also be revitalized. One of them was the Journal Square Arts District.

Looking forward to five years, Steven expressed with confidence that Journal Square would once again be the heart of the city and a well-known arts/culture destination for New York City and New Jersey residents. He made two large investments that would ultimately serve as major catalysts for the entire area. Creating two major "anchor institutions "for the arts in a one-block radius of mass transit and journal square would be the most significant change for Journal Square in the last 50 years. However, with such change, the need to examine public safety became needed.

Public Safety is amongst our most important responsibilities and Steven has continued to build upon the work of our first several years in restructuring the Jersey City Police Department towards a better more accountable and transparent department. His goal was ad continues to be consistent for a safer City for all residents, in all wards, and all neighborhoods. Also, having a Police Department that would be accountable and transparent to reflect the diversity of the City was essential, this included having a professionally led department that would be led to continued improvement for the betterment of its officers and the communities that they served. Through police reform efforts, decreases in crime numbers, and safer communities, Steven has been able to see favorable change.

For the last three years, Jersey City's shooting incidents have dropped below 90 and the total homicides have dropped below 20 under Steven's leadership. In 2019, Jersey City had a record-tying low of 13 homicides, which included four in a single active shooter event. After the pandemic hit, causing our resources were both depleted and where diverted, showing Jersey City maintained most of its reduction in violence and avoided the large increases seen in most other cities in the United States.

As crime dropped, Steven developed Jersey City to also become an economic engine for New Jersey. As the regional leader in economic growth and strength, the city's local economy has experienced unprecedented job creation, wage and compensation growth, and base expansion. Our thriving local communities are our neighborhood business districts, with over 500 new small businesses opening over the last seven years. We have seen record levels of housing units under construction in Jersey City, with over 10,000 built during the previous five years and nearly 18,000 new units approved and shovel-ready. The new housing development rate, including affordable housing and mixed-income projects, will ensure it can absorb new residents without substantial rent increases.

Through stable taxes, Steven and his administration analyzed every tax dollar to ensure the greatest efficiency without any additional burden to the taxpayers. Over his years in office, he has delivered no tax increases on the municipal side in six out of the eight budgets Steven has adopted. Few municipalities in New Jersey can compare to this record of no tax increases despite increased costs every year.

Through sound fiscal planning and management, Moody's acknowledged Jersey City's material economic and financial impact with its proximity to the United States pandemic epicenter. They reported that the city government took decisive action to address both the city's public health needs and its budgetary implications. By recognizing that stability in finances is important to our city and that's why Steven created the Department of Finance to aggregate all budgetary-related offices to find efficiencies. As a result, the budget provides funding priorities that produce the lowest crime rates in city history, new affordable housing resources, expanded critical health services, and the most extensive police and fire departments in decades.

Even as the Pandemic gripped society, Steven developed a Pandemic Management System. Jersey City was amongst the first in the country and first in the state to put restrictions and curfews in place to keep residents safe. Jersey City provided relief and resources wherever possible for its community, from grants for local businesses to a rent and utility relief program for residents through free local testing, taking action to protect residents, and maintaining transparency and data for accountability of their efforts. The city had its first BikeJC program. Steven and his administration implemented a comprehensive Bike Master

Plan that includes a complete protected bike lane system and then started to implement the steps to create a safe environment with miles of safe corridors. Steven developed meaningful steps to redesign our city streets so that as a city, they would be a leader concerning bike infrastructure. This included the city putting into place the first bike share system in New Jersey and has since expanded the system to six hundred bikes and fifty docking stations across the city, creating a new transportation system is never easy. It is especially challenging when the New Jersey government is structured in a way that cities don't control their bus, ferry, or PATH systems. It has been his interest that by 2026, an investment into a Vision Zero program, would work to accomplish zero fatal crashes within the city. The Vision Zero plan has made meaningful changes already to our streets from road diets, to speed humps, to traffic redirection, to complete street redesign.

With a commitment to a more comprehensive focus on housing for residents. This meant for Steven worked closely with the Jersey City Housing Authority leadership to create a better pathway for these residents toward more meaningful opportunities. Through Early Child Education Centers, Resident Services, Health and Wellness, Workforce Development, Food Security programs, Youth

Programming, Digital Inclusion, and Sustainability; Steven is providing for some of the most vulnerable residents when it comes to services and resources while creating opportunities for these residents towards more meaningful opportunities. This includes Health and Human Services, where Jersey City has been a leader with regard to reinforcing the importance of healthier diets in the habits of our residents. Access to food and education has been a priority for this administration. Under Steven, Jersey City created the Division of Food & Nutrition to focus on reducing hunger & food security, increasing the consumption of healthier foods amongst residents, and supporting the local food system.

Since taking office, there has been a renewed commitment to investing and providing help to some of our most vulnerable residents in a dignified way by helping the homeless residents. In spring 2021, Jersey City broke ground on the construction of a new homeless shelter with housing and social service resources bundled together. This will be the first major shelter investment the city has made in decades. Jersey City partnered with the Jersey City Housing Authority to construct a new resource drop-in center for homeless residents with services ranging from permanent shower facilities and free laundry, to expanding case management operations and mental health services.

As the nation's most diverse city, Steven is setting a new standard for how local governments can empower newcomers through immigration affairs. Jersey City is the only city in the United States to provide federally accredited immigration legal services for citizenship, Green Cards, status adjustments, travel documents, and more. In 2017, Steven worked closely with the ACLU to re-establish Jersey City as a city that will serve all of its residents that reside in the city. As a commitment to make the city healthier and safer, Steven recognized that trust with the community is paramount and as a result of that arbitrarily accepting directions from the federal government to break up families was not something that the local government would participate in. This includes maintaining sustainability within the city by investing in green spaces within the City is about more than just a commitment to protect the environment. Instead, it was about a commitment to the communities that surrounded them. Living in a densely populated city such as Jersey City, parks provide places for children to play, neighbors to meet, and communities to thrive. Understanding the importance that sustainability had on the City. By the summer of 2021, The Climate Action Plan was developed for city residents.

Focusing on energy, transit, waste, infrastructure, and municipal operations, Steven brought Jersey City into a new frontier by developing a compositing system that would reduce waste, which included a plastic bag ban. Both initiatives have made a difference in the lives of residents within Jersey City. It was through Steven's plastic bag ban initiative that this endeavor put pressure on the State of New Jersey to implement its plastic bag ban in November of 2019, but his commitment to improving lives didn't stop there. Other initiatives, such as city electric cars by the year 2030, prioritizing a newly formed Shade Tree Commission, where the city has started a semi-annual "adopt a tree" program, through which we planted over 550 trees on public property in 2020, along with investing for the future by improving the efficiency and reliability, so that the City meets its climate goals and becomes more resilient to future storm events and creating a cutting-edge micro-grid that integrates solar power, battery storage, and EV system for city-wide services by achieving its goal of 100 percent renewable energy for its municipal facilities; Steven continues to invest in the people. This includes building opportunities for youth.

Investing in tomorrow starts today. Steven has prioritized the next generation with resources to learn, grow and succeed by reshaping the way the City engages with younger residents to guarantee that our youth are provided with opportunities to grow and develop their physical and athletic needs as well as social, ethical, emotional, and cognitive competencies. Building physical schools and constructing new facilities for inner city youth across NJ, while doing it at no additional cost to taxpayers.

Developing quality programming and educational services for young people has been a priority for Steven. Despite the Jersey City Board of Education is an autonomous elected body with an independent budget, Steven has made unprecedented monetary contributions to support the schools. Steven has taken the approach that they are unwilling to write a "blank check" for any program but when there is a clear overlap with city resources the city will do all it can to help. Over the last several years, Steven has committed 14 million dollars towards lead remediation in public education facilities, and more than 7 million dollars in shared services with the city government to alleviate some of the financial responsibilities of the elected school board. Furthermore, Steven allowed more than $10 million in formerly tax-abated properties to be moved to conventional taxes to better support the traditional public schools. Other developments such as instituting a Summer Internship program was initiated the Jersey City Summer Internship Program: a partnership between the City, Jersey City Economic Development Corporation, Jersey City Public Schools, and City's leading private and non-profit firms and institutions that place high-performing high-school juniors in paid work-based learning opportunities to gain hands-on experience and provides professional enrichment and mentoring support. Every year since 2015, high-performing high school students are placed in paid internships via a partnership with the business community giving students for the first time exposure to a new corporate environment and access to new mentors.

Along with instituting a summer internship program, Steven launched a training program for high school-aged youth centered on restorative community justice and civic engagement that also assists in diverting youth from the school-to-prison pipeline and reducing suspension rates; focused on peer-led tools that develop early interventions to help prevent young people from becoming entangled in the criminal justice system, communicate effectively, and advocate for themselves and others. The program commits thousands of hours– by youth – that connect and empower youth in our community in areas such as Intergenerational social interactions/support; Community clean-up; Homeless and needy services; Food insecurity; and Mentoring/tutoring. Keeping the youth in meaningful work experiences has been important to him. Creating opportunities to gain work experience at Summer Camps, Sports Leagues and Clinics, Pools, Parks, and Maintenance has been helping to support youth, while simultaneously fulfilling important City seasonal work needs. This includes working to expand recreation programs and training for employees in mental health, grief counseling, training to inform on warning signs of suicidal tendencies in youth and child abuse/neglect, communication methods to inform residents about youth programs, and Special Needs training to educate and improve staffs' abilities to identify, include, and support, youth.

Investing in Jersey City with an unprecedented amount of money, not for the short-term, but rather through long-term infrastructure has been achieved since Steven has been mayor. It has been critical to keeping Jersey City a desirable place for current and future residents to live by building more open space, protecting bike lanes, improving sewer systems, completing upgrades to government buildings and offices, and providing services to migrate floods, that include re-routing of storm water and large pumping systems in flood-prone areas. Recognizing the importance that city services have not been the only area that Steven has made a priority for Jersey City. He has also recognized the importance of small businesses as being the backbone of the city. Small businesses are a part of the local economy since they employ city residents and help their residents with access to vital services. There is much to consider when looking back to what Jersey City was like twenty years ago to where the city is now. Improvement can be seen in every area, but there is only so much that can be done in one place, and there is still much more that can be accomplished to make not only Jersey City better, but New Jersey as well.

In April 2023, Steven announced his run for New Jersey Governor two and half years before the election partly to build grassroots support for his candidacy. For anyone hoping to win a gubernatorial primary, gaining county party support is critical to winning the coveted "line," or preferred ballot position with organization-backed candidates, with the realization that he may have to run "off the line" in some areas of the state. In his initial run for governor in 2017, some structural mistakes were made by relying only on the chairs and the structure that exist from the top down. At the time, he was convinced, and even convinced myself at the same time, that that was probably the only way to do it, and it was a mistake. However, with a different focus, he is pledging to focus on the issues facing New Jersey and its people, as Steven's leadership and accomplishments are seen across political channels and have received endorsements from mayors and labor unions alike.

Mayors serve on the front lines of each community and they have an understanding of the type of progress that is possible when given additional resources and innovative policy solutions from the state government, especially as municipalities throughout our state continue to face, particularly those related to transportation, affordability, and responsible economic development. Mayors have an opportunity to be on the ground floor developing the policy agenda that could shape the future of New Jersey. This is what is believed that Steven will pursue as the next Governor of New Jersey. His focus now is not only building up grassroots support but also putting together detailed ideas on how he'd govern. Steven believes that the Democratic primary base rewards you for substantive policies. The goal is to run a campaign that's not just going to be kind of platitudes. In broad terms and response to questions about current policies, some would build off what he's done in Jersey City, such as building housing and raising the minimum wage.

At a time when we still see small business closures on just about a daily basis, and with another year of no small business relief in the budget amid the highest business tax and regulatory burdens in the nation, it's important to recognize that every dollar does count for these folks. However, even a higher minimum wage doesn't get families too far in New Jersey because the state, like all others, severely lacks affordable housing.

While that is a complex problem to solve, Steven believes a promising start would be resurrecting the state Council on Affordable Housing. The agency was responsible for setting municipal housing requirements, among other things, but the state Supreme Court declared that it hasn't been properly functioning. This comes after years of stalled work and lawsuits. Despite any progress, New Jersey consistently faces a housing crisis, which makes it unaffordable for working families. Steven has brought Jersey City to gain attention on its approach to housing, such as the redevelopment of Holland Gardens.

His experience working with the state's programs at the local level would give him a unique understanding of how to deal with housing because he's been dealing with it at the local level, the first level of government.

By the summer of 2023, an announcement is anticipated that will present the most expansive and detailed policy agenda ever seen in a gubernatorial primary. Since Steven's success as mayor of the state's second-largest city will give him a practical understanding of how decisions in Trenton impact the day-to-day lives of taxpayers, this is what makes him uniquely well-equipped to serve the state. Steven believes that voters reward campaigns that are thoughtful around public policy and present more than just the same basic platitudes they are used to seeing. His plan is to showcase a strong record in Jersey City and a detailed plan for all of New Jersey.

From his time serving as a U.S. Marine to being Mayor of Jersey City, he has been guided by a strong desire to improve the lives of people will ultimately set him apart from others who have served in public office. The values that Steven has progressed have made a favorable impact on Jersey City and his compassion to serve others with a strong sense of values can only help the people of New Jersey in the long run, and open the door to a no strings attached way of governing New Jersey that will not only make a positive impact on the lives of the people today but for the future and beyond. In essence, the outcome would be one of a progressive movement that will transform politics with a no strings attached philosophy of governing.

About the Author

Dr. Cristina Guarneri has worked on political campaigns since 1993. She has provided seminars on Ethics and Leadership in Public Policy, including her newest seminar Ethics in Government: Looking for the Modern Abraham Lincoln. Dr. Guarneri holds a doctorate in Leadership, Management, and Policy with a concentration in Public Policy from Seton Hall University, South Orange, NJ, and a professional certification in Public Performance Measurement: Government Affairs from Rutgers University, Newark, NJ. She holds an M.F.A. and M.A. in Creative Writing and English, along with a certification in Professional Writing from Southern New Hampshire University.

Dr. Guarneri writes a column on various topics on government and current events. She is the author of the fiction books *El Shaddai, House of Deception, Almost Never Made, Wintervale Island,* and *Abington Square.* She is also the author of the non-fiction books *Veil of Secrecy, Twitterocracy,* and *Twitterocracy: Democracy through Social Media.*

Politics is not an end, but a means. It is not a product, but a process. It is the art of government. Like other values, it has its counterfeits. So much emphasis has been placed upon the false that the significance of the truth has been obscured and politics has come to convey the meaning of crafty and cunning selfishness, instead of candid and sincere service.

— Calvin Coolidge

www.ingramcontent.com/pod-product-compliance
Lightning Source LLC
Chambersburg PA
CBHW020317290526
45785CB00007B/2828